D1201875

# SO YOU WANT TO GO INTO JOURNALISM

*Other Books in This Series*

# So You Want to Go into Journalism

*by* LEONARD EAMES RYAN
*and* BERNARD RYAN, Jr.

HARPER & ROW PUBLISHERS
NEW YORK, EVANSTON AND LONDON

PN4797
R9

SO YOU WANT TO GO INTO JOURNALISM. Copyright © 1963 by
Leonard Eames Ryan and Bernard Ryan, Jr. Printed in the
United States of America. All rights reserved. No part of this
book may be used or reproduced in any manner whatsoever with-
out written permission except in the case of brief quotations
embodied in critical articles and reviews. For information address
Harper & Row, Publishers, Incorporated, 49 East 33rd Street,
New York 16, N. Y.

FIRST EDITION

B—N

LIBRARY OF CONGRESS CATALOG CARD NUMBER: 62-14567

FOR MAMMA AND DADDY

OCT 8 1963

# *Acknowledgments*

WE ARE INDEBTED to a great many of the men and women of journalism who have talked with us, written to us, or made their speeches and other writings available for use in the preparation of this book. While there are too many to mention all of them here, we do wish to express our very special appreciation to Miss Carol Lois Boggs, who assisted with our research, interviewed several of our sources, and visited the U. S. Army Information School at Fort Slocum on our behalf. She also typed all of the final manuscript.

# Contents

# *Introduction*

IT IS A BIG JOB today to try to tell the
rest of the world what is going on in some corner of it.
This is the task of the men and women of journalism,
every day, every hour, from every corner of the world
they can reach.

This book is meant to tell you, as an aspiring journalist,
something of the demands on your abilities that you will
meet as a worker in the modern web of communications
that wraps the world. It is not a textbook. Our purpose
is to try to help you to understand the opportunities
and the problems that you will face in the business.

First we will show you some journalists at work. Then
we will step into the wide world of journalism, both past
and present. Next will come some discussion of the journalist's mental outlook, followed by a chapter on those who
gather and write the news, those who edit it, the many specialists in journalism, and the publisher and those who
occupy the business office. Finally, we offer some advice for
those who are starting out, and we look a little at the
future.

It may be true that nothing is as dead as yesterday's news. We feel that nothing is more alive for our purposes than examples of the news itself. So here and there we have used actual news stories to illustrate what we have to say. For the most part, they involve events that occurred while this book was being prepared.

Journalism is a field that appeals to young people and there are many young people in it. Once they have experienced the excitement of telling the news as it happens, they usually become pretty deep in their dedication to it. Of course the world is crazy, and journalism is no exception to that. But you don't really have to be a little nuts to want to make journalism your career. Nowadays, it won't hurt if you're a little bright. We hope this book will help to make the point.

# ONE

## *What Is Journalism?*

IN MANHATTAN's Peter Cooper Village, a fourteen-year-old boy edits and publishes a sixteen-page news magazine. In Poughkeepsie, New York, a twenty-one-year-old college student has edited and published a weekly newspaper so successfully that he has pressed for designation as the town's official publication—with the town's legal advertising, worth some $5,000 a year, at stake.

Probably you have not gone this deeply into journalism as yet. But you may have grazed at the edge of the field, by delivering newspapers or selling magazine subscriptions. And, if you have not gone into journalism, certainly it has reached out to you. All your life, newspapers, magazines, radio and, for most of your life, television have been spreading the news and telling you what was going on in the world.

Probably you know a journalist or two. If you live in a small town, he is the editor of the weekly paper or one of its reporters. He is as much a part of the community as the druggist, the supermarket manager, the banker or policeman or schoolteacher. But journalism is more than the weekly paper, and the journalist is more than its reporter or editor. Journalism includes many fields and many ways of supplying information to the public, and journalists are people of many talents and abilities.

One thing the journalist today is *not:* He is not a fast-talking, hard-as-nails guy with a press card in his hatband and a bottle in his desk drawer who can lead the cops through their own misjudged clues to the criminals' hideaway and stop the presses in time to get the story on page one. He is almost none of the stereotypes you have seen in the movies or in television's situation dramas, and he does very few of the *cliché* things you may have seen him do.

Not that the journalist's life isn't often fast-paced and full of adventure. But the pace and pressure come not so much from scoring beats or scoops as from the simple fact that there is nearly always more to find out and tell about than can be learned and told. The adventure comes not so much from reporting events and sudden happenings as from being on the inside of developments that are important to the interests if not the very lives of those who read or hear or watch the report. For every journalist who jets to the South Pacific to report a governor's search for his missing son, hundreds remain at home to report what the banquet speaker said about the school board's latest projects or what happened when two cars collided at Main and Elm. Let's meet some of the many kinds of journalist now.

## *The Journalists Around Us*

It is early morning on Cape Canaveral. A tall young man wearing sunglasses strides toward one of the squat buildings within sight of the gantries and towering rockets. He carries a tape recorder marked "WFAA Dallas."

"Hello, Red," he says to the Air Force captain who greets him at the door.

"Morning, John," says the captain. "Got that thing wound up good?"

"Sure," replies John. He plugs in the tape recorder and begins speaking into the microphone: "A carrot-topped Air Force captain from Dallas owns the world's most expensive thumb. He's Captain Red Davis, range safety officer here at Canaveral. We've asked him to take a couple of minutes out of a mighty busy day here to tell us about his job. Captain Davis, what about that thumb of yours?"

The captain speaks into the microphone. "Well, John, during the launching, my thumb is right on this switch here. If the computer says something is going wrong—say the missile isn't running according to its program—I have to make the decision to cut off the power and blow it up."

"How does that affect the astronaut?" John asks.

"Well, it blows him on up high enough so his parachute can bring him down all right."

John continues his interview with Captain Davis, tracing his interest in electronics back to a physics teacher who is still a favorite in a Dallas high school.

After completing this interview, John will tape-record a talk with an official from a parachute manufacturer in El Paso, Texas, whose chutes return the astronaut's capsule to earth.

Then he will write up both interviews and dispatch them to his newspaper in Dallas, where they will appear as feature stories. His tape recordings will be broadcast, during the long waiting periods in the countdown tomorrow morning, over direct lines to Dallas. Thus the importance of Dallas's contributions to the space shoot will be told in stories and broadcasts developed especially for the local audience in Dallas.

John is a unique combination of experience and abilities. Because he served as a guided missile specialist in the Army, he was a natural to become an aerospace writer and reporter for a Dallas newspaper. Because this paper happened to own radio and TV stations in Dallas, John became what you might call a broadcasting newspaperman. He maintains a weekly radio program dealing with aerospace news, and a weekly television program in which he interprets news in depth. Columnist, reporter, newscaster—he is all these. But, broadly speaking, he is a journalist.

Now let's visit the UN. But we will not stop in the magnificent auditorium of the General Assembly, where the delegates have gathered to hear the Soviet foreign minister deliver an important address. Instead, we go behind the scenes. The room we enter is crowded with desks, more than two dozen typewriters, and telephones. Newspapers and loose piles of copy paper are mingled with ashtrays and pencils. From "squawk boxes" on the desks, the calm voice of a translator is rendering the foreign minister's opening remarks into English. Around the room, a dozen men sit quietly, listening, smoking. Others are gathered in groups of three and four at the door and in the corridor.

"It's here, Al!" somebody yells.

The men at the door and in the corridor are suddenly alert. The men at the desks crowd toward the door. A UN attendant moves among them. In his arms is a fast-dwindling stack of mimeographed papers: copies of the foreign minister's speech.

Now they settle at the desks. Every typewriter, every phone is taken. There is a controlled calm, yet a tingle of excitement can be felt. Every man is quickly but carefully glancing through the speech.

After a few minutes, one speaks. "It's this third paragraph on page five, isn't it? I think that's where he gets to the heart of their approach on Berlin."

"Right," says another. "But take a look at what he says about Communist China on page seven. In the light of what he said last week, this is pretty significant."

Which is the lead—the most important element, the subject of the leading sentence or paragraph in a report on the foreign minister's speech? That is the question these men are discussing. They are all members of the UN press corps. They represent newspapers and press services and broadcasting networks from all over the United States and, in fact, from many parts of the world. Though each spends the better part of his day in a building which belongs to no publisher and to no one country, each is spending his life in journalism.

A big room in a low, gray building in Philadelphia is crowded with desks, typewriters, teletype machines, and reams of paper. A young man at one of the desks is just hanging up the phone. He turns to an older man at the central desk.

"That was the *Sunbury Item*," he says. "They expect Washington to announce the appointment of the new Sunbury postmaster. You seen anything on it?"

"He called yesterday," replies the older man. "I told him we'd keep on top of it."

"Why's he so itchy?"

The older man shrugs. "That's what we're here for. He thinks he's got to keep jacking us up, I guess. Makes him feel he's getting his money's worth. Well, it might move this afternoon."

"B wire, or metro?"

"Probably B. But they might put it on the metro, with Kennedy's news conference coming up. Anyway, get it onto the state wire as fast as you can and keep him happy."

The older man? He's Philadelphia day editor for a worldwide wire service. The younger? A newsman serving on the day side, learning the importance of local names and local news to the papers his bureau serves. Their counterparts serve in bureaus all over the United States, and all are important links in the great chain of journalism.

Outside a warehouse in Charlotte, North Carolina, a young man jumps out of a taxi and hurries over to a truck. He carries a small suitcase and a briefcase. "You the fellow from the home office? You're a man of your word— right on time."

"Well, my plane was right on time," replies the new arrival as he introduces himself. "You ready to go?"

"All set. I'll stow your bag in the back of the cab. I suppose you'll want that briefcase handy."

The fellow from headquarters takes a stenographer's notepad from his briefcase and a pencil from his pocket and, as the big diesel engine turns over and the fifteen-ton tractor-trailer pulls away from the warehouse, begins jotting notes.

During the next fifteen hours, he will ride the truck to Jacksonville, Florida. He will learn everything he can about the distribution system that keeps a truck like this moving between plants and warehouses owned by the giant food processing firm that employs both him and the truck driver. He will get the "feel" of the driver's coffee consumption, anecdotes, and unusual experiences of the drivers. When he finally returns to his office and typewriter, he will sift the details as he writes a feature story for the twenty-four-page magazine which his company publishes monthly for its employees. A member of the public relations department of his firm, this "fellow from the home office" is nonetheless a working journalist.

We are in the offices of a television station in a midwestern city. Again we see the desks and typewriters and telephones we have seen in other newsrooms. But here is another kind of equipment; this man opens a heavy-duty carrying case, and checks the loading of a motion-picture camera. Another man approaches.

"You saw the assignment sheet, Bill?"

"Yeah. I didn't think they'd settle before the deadline. Well, if this strike lasts as long as that one three years ago, I'll be shooting an awful lot of footage."

"You going out there now?"

"Yup. Thought I'd get a head start. Might be some management people trying to cross the picket line about nine o'clock."

"Taking the Auricon?"

"Sure," says Bill.

"Good. I'll try to get over there about nine. Maybe we can pick up some interviews. Tom says he'll count on us for close to a full minute on the six o'clock report."

"Fine," Bill answers. "But I've got a lot of jobs on the clip for today—I won't get much time back here in the lab. I'll edit this one in the camera. Here—here's my breakdown." He shows the other man a slip of paper. "Five seconds long shot on the plant, so you can see the smokestacks are dead. Then about seven seconds of cover shot on the gate. Then I'll get about three, maybe four quick cuts on the picket line—two medium, to establish, and a couple of head shots if I can. If you're not there by then, I'll start lining up interviews. I expect the shop steward will be on the line this first day. What'd you say his name is? He's one of your best sources out there, isn't he?"

We'll leave Bill there, planning his film coverage of the strike. As you have gathered, he is a motion-picture photographer. His cohort is a reporter. Together they make a crack newsgathering team for their TV station.

A colorful parade moves down the main drag of a small town. A bizarre lineup of homemade and semiprofessional floats, ancient carriages, high-wheel bicycles, and vintage automobiles, it has all but finished creeping past the reviewing stand.

A busy-looking young lady hurries up to the rear of the stand. She carries a clipboard in one hand, a pencil in the other. "You judges decided on the winning float?" she calls up to the committee chairman.

"Just getting to it," replies the chairman. "Why don't you go see who's the queen?"

"Oh, they're as far behind schedule as you are," she answers.

Her mind is on a city editor fifty-five miles away. She is thankful she had the forethought to send him biographies on all six of the local beauties who are candidates for bicentennial queen, so that when she phones in the name of the winner he can just pick up the right one. But if the committee doesn't hurry up and settle the prize for the best float, and then get on to judging which of thirty-odd male candidates has grown the handsomest full beard for this momentous occasion, her two most colorful stories will miss the deadline for the last edition of the evening paper in the city—after the editor had assured her he'd want close to a column each on the parade, the queen, and the beards.

And with her husband driving one of the floats and sporting one of the beards, she has to keep track of two small children who are parked with a friend somewhere in

the crowd. As the festivities drag on into lunchtime, they'll
be announcing their hunger.

She has a lot to keep track of, this young lady. But
she wouldn't trade this part-time job for any other in the
world. It's a small but steady source of extra income for
her, and it keeps her from sinking into a world of baby
food and runny noses. She's pleased and proud to be the
town stringer for the city paper. And although she probably never stops to think about it, she is part of the lifeblood of journalism.

Halfway around the world, in a high-ceilinged room
where crystal chandeliers and plush draperies set the tone,
a highly select audience greets a lithe young model. She
crosses a low stage, turns, crosses again—and the latest
creation of Paris's most sensitive designer is news.

Among those present is a trim young lady from America.
She is a reporter for an important newspaper in New
York—but it is not a newspaper that the average New
Yorker is likely to buy or read. It is called *Women's
Wear Daily*, and it is published for a highly specialized
readership: those who design, manufacture, and sell
women's clothing.

Our young reporter is pleased to see how closely she
predicted the "line" this designer would take for next
fall. Her analysis of opinions in trade circles in New York,
combined with what she was able to gather from several
reliable sources here in Paris, has enabled her to prepare
her readers for this development. And in supplying an
accurate background that readies her special audience

for today's news, she has demonstrated that she is a skillful and competent journalist.

"Whether we like it or not, we've got to make the change." The man who is speaking sits at a well-littered desk in the far corner of the office of a weekly newspaper, in a building which was once a private home and which is shared with a real estate firm. Gathered near the desk are half a dozen men and women—the entire staff of the paper.

"Lot of people won't like it," says one of the women.

"They'll get used to it. They're buying the paper for our content, not because we look cute and small-townish. And we can't keep running those eight-column mats sideways across a spread. Besides, we've only got so many spreads to run them across—and I don't want to say no to any client just because we run an odd-ball size. So—my mind's made up." He tosses a sheet of typed paper across his desk. "I'm going to run this editorial announcing the change this week, and next week we'll go to a standard eight-column width. Just like the big boys."

So a small-town weekly paper grows a little. Its editor makes hundreds of decisions every week—not all of them as major as a change in the paper's page size—for on his shoulders fall all of the responsibilities that are shared by many individuals in a larger organization. If his weekly paper is thriving, you may be sure it is because he is not only a good editor but a sound businessman—as well as a dedicated journalist.

It is 4:30 P.M. in New York City. On the fifth floor of a

building the size of a city block, a group of men gather around a large oval table in a conference room. They carry odd shaped sheets of paper clipped together. One puts down several pencils and a good-sized eraser beside a large sheet of paper on which are diagramed eight columns, like a blank newspaper page.

One of the men seems to be teasing another. "Hello, Tom," he says. "Your presence here mean the Yanks have clinched it this afternoon?"

Tom draws on his pipe. "They're ahead five to three—last of the eighth."

The man at the head of the table turns to the one beside him. "We'll get this one out of the way in a hurry. Give Tom three inches in that lower left-hand corner." He looks across the table. "But don't go away, Tom. They can still lose it between now and the end of our meeting. And we all want to see the look on your face if they do."

Tom, who now shrugs off the round of laughter that circles the table, is sports editor of one of New York's major morning newspapers. "Come on, Charlie," he answers, "can't I at least have the lower *right?*"

Charlie, the managing editor, moves quickly to other matters. He asks the city editor about a three-way battle between the mayor, the traffic commissioner, and the parks commissioner. He checks the telegraph editor on whether an international wire service carries any greater breadth of information about the situation in the Congo than the report from the paper's own correspondent.

"Now, where's the Washington schedule?" he asks next. "Is the President's bill on housing reported out?"

A voice from across the table answers. "It's on the floor. The House hasn't adjourned yet. I talked to Wally about half an hour ago. He expects the vote at about 5:30. He doesn't see any delay at this point."

Charlie looks down at the eight-column diagram. "All right. Unless there's some dissension, let's go with that."

The man beside Charlie picks up a pencil, deftly sections off two columns of the upper right-hand corner of his diagram, and scribbles the word "President" into the space. The front page of tomorrow morning's newspaper has begun to take shape. And the other major news stories of the day follow onto this "dummy" in the order of their importance and relationship to each other.

Day in, day out, this group of editors meets at 4:30 to decide which news stories merit front-page position the next morning. Their number and membership varies slightly, including the sports editor when a pennant is won or a world record broken, or the obituary editor when a national or a world figure dies, or the business and financial editor when giant railroads merge. While the managing editor carries final responsibility for the decisions, each is amply qualified to participate—frequently with considerable heat—for each has had many years of sound experience in journalism.

### The Common Denominators

We have met just a handful of the many practitioners in the field of journalism. Already you may see that one or another of them does the kind of work you would like to do. As we go into greater detail, you will see that jour-

nalism comes in many sizes and shapes, and that the
qualifications you must bring to it, and the rewards and
satisfactions you may gain from it, are also of many
dimensions. Let's try to find the common denominators of
all who are in journalism.

The key word which holds them together is *communication.* Whatever special field he is in, the journalist belongs
to the broader field of communications. This is a vast cate-
gory of the business world, including all the forms of publication and broadcasting through which we transmit ideas
to our fellowmen. The journalist's function is to communicate news and information. He tells what is going on in the
world: what is about to happen, what is happening, and
what has just happened. He tells what people do and feel
and think. He reports. The timely and the topical are his,
for journalism is the record of history as it happens and,
in fact, before the particular event is over.

This timeliness is what gives journalism another of its
common denominators: the excitement of being in on things
as they happen or before they happen. And this excitement
leads to the common denominator of responsibility: While
the journalist may be employed by any one of a dozen or
more categories of the vast communications industry, his
responsibility is, in the final analysis, to his reader, his
viewer, or listener—the public itself.

The chief common denominators are the gathering and
dissemination of news and information. This means simply
that as a journalist you must both get the story and tell it.

Getting the story is hard work. It may mean digging out
facts. It may mean research and interviews and conjecture

and hunch and good luck. Often it means using generous amounts of an old-fashioned word in journalism: *enterprise*. If you are a reporter, enterprise means poking into things. If you are an editor or publisher, it means sending the men and spending the money to poke into things. It was a newspaper's enterprise which cracked open the facts on police corruption in Denver in 1961; it was a press secretary's enterprise which arranged the exclusive interview of Khrushchev's son-in-law with the President of the United States early in 1962.

Most "hard news"—the police stories, the natural disasters of fire, flood, or earthquake, the auto and plane crashes—usually has happened by the time the journalist starts to get the story. This is why bad news is the best news to so much of journalism: It requires a minimum of enterprise to develop bad news into sensational news. And the supply of hard news is unlimited.

Once the background material has been rounded up, there comes an equally hard job: writing the story. Here the ability to organize the material and sift the important from the trivial is second only to the ability to write plain good English that tells the story clearly and succinctly.

And the next common denominator is editing and being edited. In every area of journalism, there is always more to tell the audience than your medium can possibly accommodate. So every story must be weighed against every other story to see which comes first in the newscast or lands on page one, and to see which merits a full column or a mere paragraph. To be the editor who makes such decisions by the dozen each day, you must be equipped with a comprehensive grasp of current events, seasoned with objectivity and historical perspective, plus an intimate knowledge of the audience for whom you are editing.

In journalism, the *deadline* is everything. Whether you are a cub reporter calling in details of how much apparatus responded to a fire alarm or the drama critic of the *New York Times* reviewing a new play, you have only so many minutes in which to work. Frequently your lead is snatched from you and is on its way to the composing room or the teletype machine before you have finished the story. If you are an editor, news is coming at you fast from many directions and you have to sift through it and make decisions quickly and surely. In newspaper work, the deadlines come as often as the number of daily editions; in broadcasting, every hour on the hour; at the wire service, every minute.

Withal, it is your job to turn out clear, concise writing. You must be able to think well and fast on your feet from a phone booth or from your seat in the slot at the copy desk. You must be willing to go with what you've got even when you know that in another five minutes you might add more detail to the story or brighten the writing or pick up some more information from another source.

At the afternoon papers, you know that once the middle of the morning has passed only the most important stories will make it into the paper—and few stories are accommodating enough to break before midmorning. At the morning papers, the pace may be more leisurely because the late editions are being prepared while the world is supposedly quieting down for the night. At a radio or TV station or network, the pace builds toward the news-laden period from six to seven-thirty in the evening, slackens a while, and builds again for eleven o'clock. But the journalist who works on the air has one advantage: He can stay at his typewriter until the last possible moment, stepping into the studio while his newscast is being introduced.

Close to deadline, rewritemen and copyreaders who work well under pressure are given the breaking stories. And when a big story breaks the copy must roll out fast. A million dollar fire, a disastrous flood, or a deadlocked political convention doesn't pause while newsmen go out to dinner or catch up on their sleep.

## Some Hardships and Rewards

Journalism has been well known for its relatively low pay. While salary scales have increased encouragingly in recent years, they are still unexceptional for the great majority of journalists. Newspaper reporters make modest salaries, ranging upward toward a top of ten or twelve thousand dollars a year for the top men in major cities. Editors earn a little more. Reporters, rewritemen, copyreaders, and many editors on most daily papers belong to the American Newspaper Guild. Newsmen who appear on the air on networks or at large stations belong to the American Federation of Radio and Television Artists; AFTRA pay scales help to make broadcast journalists among the highest paid. Higher pay in the public relations field has been drawing the ambitious and talented from other areas, particularly newspapers, for some years now, and salaries at the news magazines, too, compare more favorably with the professions. Then there are variations depending on the city or part of the country and what your experience is. At the top of the earnings scale in journalism you will find syndicated columnists and the best known network broadcasters. It is not uncommon for these men to earn $100,000 a year. (We'll discuss money and journalism in greater detail in Chapter Nine.)

A newspaper city room is a clattering place, devoid of privacy, demanding good powers of concentration. A $25 million building may be put up by a thriving newspaper, but it is likely to forget to include any facility for the librarian to bind old issues. Cleanliness is alien to most news rooms; if you want to work at a desk not adorned with the cigarette butts and trash of an occupant from the previous shift, you probably will have to get rid of them yourself. Certain types of journalist seem to have no objection to sitting down today amid yesterday's waste paper and other litter.

Theodore H. White has given us a definitive picture of the journalist on one type of assignment, supposedly one of the most glamorous:

> The men assigned to cover a Presidential campaign are, normally, the finest in the profession of American journalism —men of seniority and experience, some of them of deep scholarship and wisdom, all of them full of dignity and a sense of their own importance. Yet for weeks and months they must live like tramps—shaken, rushed, fighting with police at police lines, dirty and unbathed for days on end, herded into buses like schoolboys. (Theodore H. White, *The Making of the President.* New York: Atheneum Publishers, 1961, p. 335.)

If newsmen are not herded, they herd themselves. If the President stops in New York to shake hands with the mayor, the biggest part of the crowd that surrounds them is newsmen. When a Rembrandt painting is sold to the Metropolitan Museum for over $2 million, the workmen can barely load it onto the truck at the auction gallery for the newsmen underfoot. When the *France* arrives on her maiden voyage, more than three hundred newsmen from all over the country come aboard with the New York harbor pilot. And newsmen may be welcome at certain times and places but not at others. Where you practically had the run of Gracie Mansion, the mayor's residence in New York, before an election, you find a few weeks later that you are confined to a basement room where a scrawled sign says, "No chauffeurs, newsmen, etc. permitted in police booth or Gracie Mansion without authorization."

Hours are odd. Some journalists go for years working the midnight to morning early shift and can't imagine anybody in his right mind wanting to sleep at night and work in the daytime. Working through the weekend, with midweek days off, may be a lifetime habit and you can go for years without being off on a major holiday like Christmas unless it falls on your regular day off. In some offices, an editor or bureau chief may hold you to the very letter of the guild contract provision for half an hour for lunch, and you will not go to lunch until you are told to. And, believe it or not, it is even possible to land in an office where you are expected to ask permission to go to the bathroom.

The journalist is traditionally thought of as a pretty tough and hard-boiled fellow, and he is likely to be treated in a tough and hard-boiled way by his own. When the *Los Angeles Examiner* was put to death in 1962, the employees on duty got the news over the paper's public address system on the day of the last edition. When the *Detroit Times* went out of business in 1960, many employees were told not to come to work next day—by telephone and telegram at three o'clock in the morning.

Then there are some other hazards of the trade. Most of these occurred within the past year: A western boots-and-saddle columnist was nearly thrown when his horse shied and ran away from the flash of a photographer's camera. A *New York Herald-Tribune* correspondent was twice taken prisoner by Irish UN troops in Elizabethville. A United States Senator punched Eric Sevareid, and General Edwin A. Walker punched a Washington reporter. Responding to a telephoned tip, a Chicago reporter fell into a trap set by thugs who left him with four razor slashes in the face. Covering the Los Angeles forest fires, a reporter and photographer were bombed by borate dropped from a plane, while another reporter burned his fingers picking up a trophy from the ashes of Joe E. Brown's home. Of about forty reporters and photographers covering the fighting at Bizerte, two were wounded—a rate of attrition as high as among the French troops in the skirmish. In McComb, Mississippi, four young men attacked three newsmen who were in town on assignment, knocking one through a plate glass window; three days later, the sixty-one-year-old editor and publisher of the McComb *Enterprise-Journal* was beaten in broad daylight on the main street. In France, it took the police to break it up when

Brigitte Bardot's friends attacked interview-determined newsmen. And two newsmen covering Governor Rockefeller's search for his missing son in New Guinea learned, as they departed, that in bartering for souvenirs they had inadvertently purchased native women.

One of the greatest rewards in journalism is simply that you go places and do things you would never do in any other walk of life. One story may take you into the psycho ward of a hospital, another to a governor's home for tea, a third to the White House for a concert by Pablo Casals, a fourth to Ireland for the inauguration of a new airline— all of which happened to one young reporter in a rather short time on general assignment for a specialized publication. And this young reporter was a woman.

Journalism has a complex personality. It is a high calling, peopled with idealists and cynics, geniuses and dullards. It is a purposeful institution dedicated, in the ideal, to meeting the people's need to be informed. It demands dedication in the individual. Call it business, trade, or profession, it offers you an exciting, lazy, frustrating, demanding, sloppy, rewarding way of life.

# TWO

## *The Wide World of Journalism*

ON A THURSDAY AFTERNOON, a man who has finished his day's work stops to buy his favorite news magazine. Driving home, he hears an hourly newscast on the car radio. He picks up the evening newspaper from the front steps. In the living room, he notices that the six o'clock news is just coming on television.

With the exception of the purchase of the news magazine, it is possible for this scene to be duplicated more than 46 million times every day in America, for there are more than 46 million television receivers in this country. We buy 58 million newspapers every day. We own 149 million radios. And we purchase a yearly total of over 300 million magazines.

We are all aware that newspapers and magazines, and television and radio are the principal means by which we get the news. But each of these media of communication is a vast world itself, and together they make up the wide world of journalism. And when we remember that journalism is the gathering and dissemination not only of news but of information, that world widens even more.

How wide is it, and to what extent does it reach into our lives? This chapter will try to give you a broad picture of its scope, its history and function. We will be talking now not so much of the journalist and what he does as of the means of communication and what they do.

## *The Media: Communications*

Whatever the news and information medium, and whatever its size, it appeals to a definable audience. With the exception of one publication, the United States has no national newspapers (as England has). Network news, broadcast to the entire country at once, occurs but once or twice a day on television and radio. A handful of news magazines may boast circulations so large and appeal so general as to refute this premise. But by and large every newspaper, every radio or TV station, every magazine represents a certain field.

With rare exceptions, the field is geographical in the case of newspapers and broadcasting: It covers a certain number of square miles in certain directions. In the case of magazines, on the other hand, the field is mostly defined by economics and by interests: Certain magazines appeal more to one income group than to another, or to special tastes or cultures. Yet there are variations in each of these categories: the *Wall Street Journal*'s field has nothing to do with geography, while *Sunset* magazine is published only for those who live on the West Coast.

The medium of publication serves the field and derives its support from it. Its service and its support depend upon the composition of the population in its field, the resources of the area (whether geographic or economic or cultural) and its entire business structure. The audience may be blue collar or white collar workers; the area may be resort town or college town; suburban neighborhood of homes and shops or complex, traffic-choked metropolis; the subject may be sports and outdoor activities or literature and stereo records; Sunday afternoon's old movies or Sunday afternoon's discussion programs—the characteristics of the field are never exactly the same for any two media. And as a journalist it is your job to know the characteristics of the field with which you are communicating, whether you work for a newspaper, magazine, or broadcasting station.

Let's look more closely now at these three basic media. And, while we're at it, we'll examine a fourth—the press association or wire service—which serves and derives its support from the other three.

## *The Newspaper*

Traditionally, the daily newspaper has been the backbone of journalism. It compiles the permanent record of history as it happens, brought up to date every twenty-four hours. Eighty-eight per cent of American families buy one or more newspapers every day, and more than 125 million adults read a paper daily.

Impressive figures? Perhaps—until you learn that in the entire country only 1,761 daily newspapers are published, that 50 papers have disappeared since 1957, that 94 per cent of our cities contain no competitive papers (some offer morning and afternoon papers separate and distinct in name, but with a single ownership), that in 20 of our states no city has competitive papers, that in each of 11 other states only one city offers competitive papers. While 125 million adults read a paper daily, very few of them have any real degree of choice about *what* paper they read.

Journalism teachers were recently asked to name the nation's ten best newspapers, judging them "on the basis of comprehensive gathering of the news, objective treatment of it, judgment in the selection of it, layout and typography, good writing, and accuracy, in that order." (*The Saturday Review,* May 13, 1961, p. 60.) The *New York Times* led all the rest, with votes from 71 per cent of those surveyed, followed by the *Christian Science Monitor* and the *Wall Street Journal.* Among the top fifteen, all except two were papers located in the northeast quadrant of the country. While the *Times* is geographically a New York paper, its circulation is so extensive (including special Paris and Los Angeles editions) that it has become the nearest thing we have to a national daily paper. And since the next two ranking papers in this survey both appeal to non-geographic or special-interest fields (the *Monitor* is a general newspaper, but its readership is special-interest), it is obvious that top-notch newspapers are sprinkled around the country less generously than first division major league ball clubs.

Three quarters of American newspapers arrive at the home via the delivery boy; they are bought by regular subscribers. And nearly three quarters of the people read the paper thoroughly, while one quarter quickly scan.

Reading increases from 70 per cent among those with less than $3,000 annual income, to 95 per cent for those who earn above $10,000, according to one survey. And when asked, "Which do you feel closest to—radio, TV or newspapers?"—40 per cent of readers answered "newspapers" while TV got 33 per cent. (American Newspaper Publishers Association and American Association of Newspaper Representatives.)

For all this devotion and habit, what does the reader of the big daily newspaper get? He gets whole pages of advertising unpunctuated by news; the ratio of news columns to advertising columns has been declining steadily for some years now. He gets entertainment of all kinds, from comic strips to gossip columnists. He gets less and less real news and information about his neighborhood or community. And much of the news he gets about the world beyond his own city comes in the form of syndicated columns.

The result is that, if you begin to read about the newspaper situation today (as you surely must if you are interested in journalism), you will soon discover that everybody is talking about "the death of American newspapers." What is causing the death? Competition from other media, mainly television. Rising costs of gathering as well as printing the news. Even the late-afternoon traffic jam, stymieing the fast movement of newspaper delivery trucks, is a factor in many cities. But more than these, perhaps, is the fact that many big city newspapers have failed to keep abreast of the field they serve and are supported by. As cow pastures have become suburbs and suburbs have become communities, a whole new field has grown up, declared its independence, and taken over one section after another.

More than 2,000 strictly suburban newspapers are now published, and the number grows almost daily. You can find 230 community papers in greater Los Angeles, 23 of them dailies; Chicago's community papers number 161; the five boroughs of New York alone support 60. And in the last ten years, while New York papers lost 2,794,144 circulation, the suburban papers in Connecticut, New Jersey, and New York state suburbs of the city grew by 42 per cent. To nearly one quarter of the American public, no other single news medium is as important as the suburban paper. Here is the daily or weekly record of history as it happens; here each local government agency, each high school team, each exchange of real estate, each luncheon-club meeting, each auto accident and brush fire and clambake and wedding and death has its importance, and here the story of each may be read and clipped and saved.

Thanks to the growth of suburban newspapering, it can be said that more daily papers were born than died in 1961, reversing a ten-year trend. And weekly papers, in the suburbs and beyond, are thriving too. Nearly 9,000 of them circulate to 75 million readers, conveying news and information that is purely local wherever it is published.

A rather special weekly phenomenon is the Sunday paper; 563 metropolitan newspapers publish Sunday editions, and 120 million readers wade into if not through them. They range upward from a dozen or more pages to the Sunday *New York Times,* which has been known to weigh in at six pounds, or 600 pages, nearly three inches thick. Sunday feature sections appeal to every interest, and exercise the talents of every kind of journalist.

America now has one national newspaper, the *National Observer,* launched early in 1962 by the *Wall Street Journal.* It is a weekly of broad general appeal covering all news that is of national interest.

Besides the general dailies and weeklies, some 2,000 publications reach out to special audiences; the *Journal of Commerce, Women's Wear Daily, Progressive Grocer, Footwear Daily,* to name a few—each gathers and disseminates news and information in a highly specialized field. Known as *trade papers,* many of them are *news*papers in a more pure sense of the word than the paper that is flung onto the average American doorstep each evening. These are the papers whose field or community of readers is economic or special-interest, rather than geographic.

Not only are many morning and evening papers under single ownership, many are owned in chains or groups. Among the best known of these are the Scripps-Howard papers, currently numbering nineteen, and the Hearst chain, now reduced to eleven newspapers and a dozen or so magazines and newspaper supplements—both nationwide chains. Regional groups range from the nearly twenty Gannett newspapers to Paddock Publications, a chain of more than a dozen weekly papers in Chicago suburbs. Altogether, more than 100 separate daily newspaper groups may be counted in the United States. Chains are strong in the trade or special-interest area, too: Fairchild

Publications gets out three dailies and four weeklies and sells 830,000 copies per week, while McGraw-Hill publishes more than 30 weekly and monthly papers and magazines for a total circulation of over 1 million.

Not to be overlooked are the Sunday supplements—magazine-like sections that appear in, although they are not produced by, your Sunday newspaper. These range from *American Weekly*, which reaches over 4 million Americans through ten papers, to *Family Weekly*, which in 200 papers reaches over 5 million. Largest circulation is held by *This Week*, read by more than 14 million through 43 papers.

## Broadcasting

In the medium we have been discussing—newspapers—the dissemination of news and information is (at least in theory) the chief *raison d'être*. Entertainment, where it appears (and plenty of it does appear), is of secondary importance as editorial content.

In the broadcasting industry, on the other hand, you communicate entertainment first, and news and information second. The majority of hours on the air are devoted to entertaining the audience, not to informing it.

The audience itself is vast. Television is now full grown; while 71 per cent of American households have vacuum cleaners, 73 per cent possess bathtubs, and 80 per cent have telephones, the total of homes with television is over 90 per cent. And 97 per cent have radios. The average home is able to receive 4.4 TV stations, out of a national total of 565 stations on the air, while a choice of 8.7 radio stations is available to the average listener, from a total of 3,376 AM and FM stations in the country.

The average American thus has a greater range of choice when he wants to look or listen than when he wants to read a newspaper.

However, many broadcasting stations are owned by newspaper publishers. Where only one daily newspaper is published and where the principal radio station is owned by that newspaper, the citizen has access to only one local news source; he can buy papers and tune in stations from nearby cities, but in their columns and broadcasts he will not get the detailed local news that he seeks about his own area.

In both radio and TV, stations are either affiliates of networks, or independents. The network-affiliated station carries network news and information programs but is expected to cover local news with its own programing. The independent station, belonging to no network, must originate all its programing.

To give you some idea of the balance of news and information programs to entertainment programs: if a station is on the air for eighteen hours a day, it broadcasts 126 hours a week; during the third quarter of 1961, the average affiliated TV station spent three hours and ten minutes a week on network news, while the average local station devoted four hours and twelve minutes a week to local newscasts.

Three or four hours out of 126—this may not seem like much, but consider that NBC's president estimated recently that hours devoted to news and informational programs in 1961 increased by 72 per cent over five years earlier. And consider the costs of gathering and disseminating news on television: NBC spends $25 million yearly on news and public affairs programs, 81 per cent of which is not recovered through charges to sponsors. By contrast, ABC, the third-ranking network, is said to have set a budget of $7 million for news director James C. Hagerty when he moved in from the White House to build up its news department.

Radio is still the ideal news medium, because it is the only medium capable of informing its audience while the news is happening. Although the communications satellite Telstar can transmit live broadcasts from Europe at certain hours, television cannot yet send an instantaneous live picture to the American audience from anywhere in the world, any time, as radio can send instantaneous live sound; a radio reporter with a microphone can go places and describe things that no TV camera can get near and at a fraction of the cost of television coverage.

With 97 per cent of the country within hearing, radio serves splendidly for getting out bulletins. Unfortunately, the bulletin has become the entire news story, and the capsule edition has become the standard newscast; it is virtually impossible to find a fifteen-minute news roundup on radio these days. The five-minute newscast is the norm, appearing regularly on the hour and the half-hour, but it has two major drawbacks: first, it is almost never five minutes long. More likely, if it is sponsored by an advertiser, it contains two minutes and fifteen seconds of news. Second, not enough news breaks every hour to provide new stories, and not enough stations are ready to spend the money to freshen the news by rewriting for each broadcast. The result is the same news in the same words in the same order over and over again.

On the other hand, its coverage of the special news event is, justifiably, broadcasting's proudest boast. When Colonel Glenn soared into orbit in February 1962, the television and radio coverage was so comprehensive that the three major networks assigned 500 people and spent over $2 million on the story. (This figure includes the cost of several delays before the takeoff.) Costs are high and getting higher, yet the special news story or report in depth is *the* bright spot in television programing.

In major stations, the newsroom is run like that of a big daily. Newsbreaks, complete with motion-picture action, can be written and produced on the air within twenty minutes after the film footage is received. NBC's "instant news specials" can give the entire country a comprehensive wrap-up of a major story within a few hours of the time the news breaks. The American Broadcasting Company has instituted a daily news program specifically directed at the teen-age audience—something no other general news medium has offered to do. Almost any *NBC White Paper* or *CBS Reports* has greater appeal than whatever is on another channel at the same time. The problem that faces broadcast journalism daily, and that will face you if you go into this area, is not how to attain quality but how to attain *quality in quantity.* News and information in quantity, but without quality, are on the air everywhere.

## The Wire Service

Much of the news and feature material that is broadcast on the air and printed in daily papers is not gathered by the stations or networks or papers themselves. It clatters into the newsroom in a machine known as a Teletype, which looks like an oversize typewriter busily typing away all by itself, usually with no keys. The machine is activated by electrical impulses sent over a telegraph wire—hence the term "wire service" for the organization which supplies the machine and gathers the news to transmit on it.

The United States news media are served by two nationwide and worldwide wire services: the Associated Press, and United Press International. These agencies serve media in other parts of the world, too, where they compete with at least two other major press agencies— Agence France Presse, whose home office is in Paris, and Reuters, of London—and many smaller agencies. (The latter have few subscribers in this country, so that competition is almost entirely between AP and UPI.) The purpose of any wire service is to provide news quickly and accurately; while it does not publish or broadcast anything itself, it must transmit material that is factual and unbiased and ready to be rushed to a composing room or studio the minute it is received, with little or no editing.

The largest newsgathering and news-distributing organization in the world is the Associated Press. A nonprofit group owned by its member papers and broadcasters, it provides news to more than 1,700 papers and 2,000 radio and TV stations, plus 4,000 users outside the United

States in a total of 80 countries. Domestic coverage of the
United States is the AP's lifeblood; a Washington staff
of 150, heavy coverage of state capitals, and special
regional service give it vast scope. Overseas, the AP
London office numbers 156, and 80 bureaus are found
around the world (not so impressive when you remember
that 104 nations are members of the UN).

United Press International is an independent, tax-
paying organization set up for profit. With a total of
about 5,800 clients, and bureaus in 85 countries, it
serves slightly fewer but with slightly broader overseas
coverage.

Both wire services supply pictures by wire; both provide
features and stories by specialists; both offer special radio
wires written to be heard rather than read. (One of the
reasons for radio's steady diet of five-minute newscasts is
that the wire services abandoned the fifteen-minute for-
mat.)

Because so many different papers and stations with so
many different local fields are served, the wire report must
be written in the plainest good English and with the least
interpretation. The wire service is just that—a service—
to its subscribers, and what it serves should be a constant
flow of unbiased fact. The flow is not only constant but
enormous; it includes, from international, national, regional, and local sources, all stories that might possibly be
of interest to editors in a given local area. This means
moving on the wire to Pennsylvania stations and papers
not only what Khrushchev says at a Geneva conference
but what the Pennsylvania governor says on a visit to

Erie; it means moving not only the story and box score on the Phils' game in St. Louis but on the Williamsport game at Jamestown. Wire service teletypes run almost constantly twenty-four hours a day, and the enormity of their flow will strike you the first time you are assigned to open an office in the morning and scoop up, rip, and sort the armfuls of paper that have ribboned out of the machine overnight.

"To cover everything newsworthy everywhere. That is our basic continuing responsibility . . ." says the editor of UPI. (*Editor & Publisher*, December 20, 1961, p. 13.) And he might have added, to supply it everywhere. When an avalanche buries three to four thousand people in Peru, when a tidal wave hits Japan or an East German soldier leaps the wall in Berlin, your paper has a picture and story the next morning because a wire service is covering everything everywhere and supplying everywhere. Joe Rosenthal's picture of the flag raising on Mount Surabachi, Iwo Jima, became the most memorable photo of World War II, not only because it was a superb picture but because he was an AP staffer at the time and the picture was immediately moved on Wirephoto everywhere. One recent study indicated that three fourths of the foreign news in American newspapers was supplied by news agencies; this is the hard core of foreign news and then some.

Like the news and information media, some news agencies serve fields that may be defined geographically or by special interest. The City News Bureau of Chicago, for instance, is one of the oldest (and one of the best training grounds for journalism—its list of alumni reads like a

Who's Who in journalism). Operating twenty-four hours a day, it serves Chicago area media with a staff that can be ready to cover any event on five-minutes' notice, and with fourteen miles of underground pneumatic tubes. And Fairchild Publications, with its many business papers to supply with specialized news and information, maintains its own wire service. Including bureaus in 29 major cities of the United States and in 37 cities around the world, with about 400 correspondents, it is the third ranking newsgathering organization in the world after AP and UPI. Even the Luce magazines are served by the Time-Life News Service, an organization of the magizine publishing company's 30 domestic and foreign news bureaus.

## *Magazines*

That brings us to the other general news and information medium: magazines. Three hundred million copies of more than 3,000 different magazines are bought each year. You can think of almost no area of human interest and endeavor for which no magazine is published. From *Mechanix Illustrated* to *True Confessions* to *Living for Young Homemakers*—about 700 general consumer magazines, plus over 2,500 business and trade magazines, account for the total. But more interesting than figures for the aspiring journalist is the fact that for several years now the contents of magazines generally have shown a steady trend away from fiction and toward bigger and bigger percentages of informational material. The circulations of the three leading news weeklies—*Time, Newsweek,* and *U.S. News & World Report*—have climbed 250 per cent since 1940. And since 1950 the "thought leader" magazines—*Atlantic, Harper's,* the *Reporter, Saturday Review*—have risen 87 per cent.

"Magazines can be abreast of the urgent issues of our day—yet remain sufficiently detached to provide background and perspective," says a former reporter named John Fitzgerald Kennedy. This is the advantage of the weekly or monthly magazine over the daily newspaper or the broadcast; its journalism is equally topical, but with the dimension which a few more days (or even a few more hours) may add to the unfolding story. Compared to the frenzy with which depth reporting or interpretation must be developed for a newspaper story, the magazine has heaps of time. And, since the reader also has more time, the magazine report may be lengthier, more comprehensive, more analytical, more authoritative. The length-of-sale period (a week or month, as the case may be) increases the demand for accuracy and depth.

While the vast majority are not "news magazines," any magazine that is not 100 per cent fiction is bound to publish material which is news to its particular audience. Some of this is "hard news" in the true sense of the word: current, up-to-the-minute, fast-breaking, whether in sports, fashions, or stamp collecting. The rest is feature or informational in quality. Sometimes the fields or audiences for different magazines overlap, and in rare cases the media overlap. With 8 million paid circulation, the biggest weekly magazine in the country could not exist without the medium it reports on, for it is *TV Guide* (and its reporting is more a verbatim transcript of station program schedules than journalism). Or look at farm magazines: Their circulation has gone steadily upward while, since 1940, we have lost more than a million farms and more than 8 million farm people. One magazine, the *New Yorker*, is an anomaly: while it is famed for its wit, urbanity, and excellent fiction, it consistently offers the finest journalism of our day—yet seems to be taken for granted in the journalism area. Furthermore, by refusing to put giveaway prices on its subscriptions, the *New Yorker* goes merrily along making money while its brothers are hoist on the petards of their circulation wars.

For magazines come and go. Generally speaking, they seem to have shorter lifetimes than newspapers. Except for the *Saturday Evening Post* and the *Ladies Home Journal*, none of the current crop of popular magazines was around when your grandmother was your age. Each year sees a few new ones, and one or two become permanent; and each year sees some disappear.

One special area of magazine publishing is the company publication. Estimates of the number of these published in America range from 4,000 to 10,000; they represent an annual investment by United States industry of about $500 million. With the cost of publication paid by a business or industry, the magazine goes free of charge to employees, stockholders, customers and suppliers, and interested friends. While some company publications are little more ambitious than the traditional "house organ," such magazines as IBM's *Think* rank with the finest specialized journals on the market.

An important thing to remember if you're heading

toward journalism: It is a fact that in areas of our country where newspapers are weak, the circulation of weekly news magazines is strong; where newspapers are strong, you will find poorer circulation of weekly news magazines.

## History of Journalism

You may think that journalism was the natural outgrowth of the development of the printing press. But a century and a half passed between the printing of Gutenberg's Bible, in 1456, and the printing of the world's first newspaper at Antwerp, Belgium, in 1605. Early newspapers in English were subject to considerable censoring and licensing by the Crown, by the Star Chamber, and by Parliament itself. But journalists of three hundred years ago were determined to publish reports of the proceedings of Parliament, often at their peril, and to exercise their right to comment on the government. In 1763, one John Wilkes got himself expelled from Parliament and subsequently imprisoned by satirizing the government, but government reporting continued to grow to the point where, in 1828, Thomas Babington Macaulay said, "The gallery in which the reporters sit has become a fourth estate of the realm," thus providing the handle by which the press has ever since been known. Freedom of the press —the right of newspapers freely to report the deliberations of Parliament—was not formally recognized by that body until 1835.

Meantime, in the American colonies, the first newspaper had appeared (and disappeared after one issue) in 1690. The *Boston News-Letter*, however, was born in 1704 and

lived to be the first newspaper to report the fighting at
Lexington and Concord in 1775. The issue of freedom of
the press was settled early and firmly in what is perhaps
the best known of all colonial trials—that of John Peter
Zenger. His acquittal on a charge of libel established the
right of the press to print what it wished, if what it
printed was the truth.

Benjamin Franklin was a highly successful journalist,
publisher, and printer; his *Pennsylvania Gazette* gained
the largest circulation in the colonies.

A journalist named Thomas Paine turned his skill at
interpretive journalism into such revolution-inspiring
pamphlets as *Common Sense* (it sold better than 300,000
copies—a not-bad-at-all run by today's standards and one
that must have been phenomenal at the time). Only the
Declaration of Independence itself played a stronger role
in creating the spirit of '76.

Newspapers at the end of the eighteenth century were
tabloid size or smaller; then, as the nineteenth century
dawned, improvements in printing machinery brought
larger and larger papers, until they became known as
blanket sheets. And for a century the weekly newspaper
thrived as our nation grew.

Journalism during the Civil War would make a book
in itself. While photographs had been taken during the
Crimean War, it remained for Mathew B. Brady to make
the camera a major tool of the journalist. And on both
sides, North and South, the free access of correspondents
to troop movements and to battle, the almost complete lack

of censorship at the source, and both governments' lack of interference with newspaper criticism, set remarkable standards.

The latter part of the nineteenth century brought the three M's: machines, magazines and Mergenthaler. Railroad and telegraph opened the West, and the United States began to exist as a single national marketplace. To reach this marketplace, magazines sprouted: The journalist began to communicate not with one locality at a time but with vast audiences, while the manufacturer advertised his machine-produced wares to this nationwide audience. But all this time, printers had set type by hand, one letter at a time (and, for that matter, copy had been written in longhand for them!). In 1886 Ottmar Mergenthaler introduced the Linotype, a machine (labeled "the eighth wonder of the world" by Thomas Edison) which mechanically casts whole lines of type as its operator strikes keys similar to those of a typewriter. The printing press grew to enormous capacities and capabilities, printing, cutting, folding, disgorging thousands of newspapers per hour. And refinements in papermaking brought ever greater rolls of newsprint to the press room at ever lower cost.

The American genius for invention was matched by the American journalist's bent for enterprise. Fame and, in some cases, wealth awaited the journalist who knew how to speak out loud and clear to his reader in the era of "personal journalism"—an era that began some time in the nineteenth century and ended some time in the twentieth (perhaps about the time Edward R. Murrow traded in

DUQUESNE UNIVERSITY LIBRARY 070.4 R988

his kind of personal journalism for an easy chair in a television studio, from which to visit the homes of celebrities).

Independent journalists of the heyday of American newspapering included men like Horace Greeley, a country boy who arrived in New York a journeyman printer in 1831 and left it in 1872 to run for President of the United States, after having founded the *New York Tribune* and built it into a million-dollar institution.

In New England, Samuel Bowles led the *Springfield Republican* to a national reputation, while later, in the South, Josephus Daniels's fame and ability as an editor led him into politics and the post of Secretary of the Navy in Woodrow Wilson's Cabinet.

In the Midwest, William Allen White bought an obscure Kansas paper, the *Emporia Gazette*. In 1895 he won fame overnight with an editorial titled "What's the Matter with Kansas?"; and by his fervid journalism he continued to command the attention and respect of the entire country until his death in 1944.

Then there were names like Joseph Pulitzer, whose *World* building was New York's tallest when it went up in 1890, and who prayed for a newspaper "forever fighting every form of Wrong," and William Randolph Hearst, who in his younger days at the turn of the century was an active and fighting liberal, who all his life understood news and how to gather it, and what kind sold papers, and who by this knowledge became the most powerful journalist of his day.

Among journalism's proudest days were those between

1900 and World War I, when magazine after magazine turned to exposing the social evils of the times, to charging corruption on the part of public men and corporations, to creating a heightened public awareness among readers— all of which was then known derisively but is now remembered reverently as "muckraking."

The recklessness of the 1920's was reflected in the rough-and-tumble journalism dramatized on the stage in *The Front Page* and in the no-holds-barred journalism that hounded the American hero, Charles A Lindbergh, from his triumph through his tragedy. Newspapers, and in some cases the quality of thought that went into them, shrank to tabloid size. Magazines sprouted to capture some of their circulation and, in the case of *Time*, avowedly to provide a weekly summary of all the news.

Radio had begun experimentally before the Great War, and its inventor, Lee de Forest, is himself credited with the first news broadcast: the announcement of the early returns in the Wilson-Hughes election in 1916. Four years later, KDKA in Pittsburgh made instantaneous reporting official with its coverage of the Harding-Cox election. Soon millions were listening regularly not only to entertainment but to news broadcasts, as radio confounded the established media by proving that any event from a base-ball game to the explosion of the *Hindenberg* could be reported as it happened, if a reporter was on the scene. (The first broadcast ball game was smuggled through a ball park telephone in 1921; the famous *Hindenberg* eye-witness report happened because a radio reporter was on the air describing what was expected to be a routine land-ing when the dirigible blew up.) And when the Japanese bombed Pearl Harbor in 1941, between three and four thousand residents of the greater New York area were equipped in their living rooms to watch several hours of continuous reports and commentary offered by the Columbia Broadcasting System over something called television.

## Freedom of the Press

The right of the press to print what it wished, reports on the proceedings of government, free access to sources and events, lack of censorship at the source and lack of interference with criticism, enterprise, personal journalism, fighting every form of Wrong, muckraking, hounding the hero, broadcasting events as they happen—what have all these in common? They have *freedom of the press*. Thomas Jefferson defined it in a letter to a friend.

The way to prevent irregular interpositions of the people [into the actions of Congress] is to give them full information of their affairs through the channel of the public papers, and to contrive that those papers should penetrate the whole mass of the people. The basis of our governments being the opinion of the people, the first object should be to keep that right: and were it left to me to decide whether we should have a government without newspapers or newspapers without a government, I should not hesitate to prefer the latter.

Jefferson's brethren defined it for all of us in the first amendment to the Constitution in 1791:

Congress shall make no law restricting an establishment of religion, or prohibition the free exercise thereof; or abridging the freedom of speech, or of the press; or the right of the people peacably to assemble, and to petition the government for a redress of grievances.

There are two important things to remember about freedom of the press as it was established in our Constitution: first, that the press is the only form of private enterprise that is specifically mentioned in and protected by the Bill of Rights; and, second, that like every other "right" protected by the Constitution, this one is not without concomitant obligations.

Thus, by the law of the land, a private business is given free access to the truth, and is entitled to seek the truth and to declare it when it is found. In all the world, there is no real source of unbiased information except the free press of our country and of those who share our ideals. The press (and for this discussion, let the word "press" include all the means of communication by which news and information are disseminated) freely and frankly tells Americans of their savage reverses during war in the Pacific, stands by with full public coverage for the launching of an astronaut, stalks the brothers of the leading contender for the nomination across the convention floor, sits in the gallery of Congress and of the courtroom, hangs around the police court to see who is booked for drunken driving.

A hundred years ago, Presidents of the United States were accustomed to giving reporters the run of the private rooms of the White House; and the President today goes out on a more dangerous limb in every White House press conference than at any other time; permitting direct quotation and "live" broadcast, he risks being lured into an untenable position on any issue of the day by any of the scores of reporters who vie for the chance to question him. By the same token, it is this peculiar character of American press freedom that makes such an extraordinary event of the President's granting an exclusive interview to the reporter son-in-law of the Russian premier, and the President's knowledge of the importance of our press freedom to the world at large, that makes the interview most effective.

Yet there are always attempts to limit the freedom of the press to investigate and report. From the White House itself came the suggestion not long ago that editors help set up a system of censorship of news related to national security, a suggestion to which a group of editors replied that the press could and would "protect information vital to national security if that information is made available . . . in an atmosphere of free access."

Recently under attack has been Canon 35 of the Canons of Judicial Ethics of the American Bar Association, which forbids the broadcasting of courtroom proceedings or the taking of photographs during court sessions or recesses. Modern reporters argue that freedom of the press is highly discriminatory when it permits a reporter whose tools are pencil and paper to be in the courtroom but bars one whose tools are camera and microphone.

A somewhat controversial aspect of freedom of the press is "privilege"—established in some states of the Union as the right of the journalist to refuse to disclose his news source. As a result of recent decisions in the United States Court of Appeals and in Hawaii Supreme

Court holding that constitutional freedom of the press does not give reporters the right to conceal news sources in legal matters, more than one newsman has gone to jail for such refusal. And in the United Nations, the General Assembly's social committee recently defeated a proposal to restrict the right of the world's journalists to search for information.

Even more important than some of these rights are the obligations which are implicit in such rights. In assuming the responsibility for "the public's right to know," the press takes on the obligation to inform, to explain, to teach. The function of news media is to publish news and, in today's light, to publish it in perspective, to organize it for understanding. In a world in which the United States has been thrust into leadership, this is an awesome obligation. It is the obligation to get and tell the public the truth, not only about the missile and space races, not only about the town meeting but about the conduct and philosophy of a new government in the Congo. It is the responsibility of the press to inform the public about the weather, the price of eggs, the cause of an airplane crash. This responsibility has never been expressed better than by the *London Times* in 1851:

The first duty of the press is to obtain the earliest and most correct intelligence of the events of the time, and instantly, by disclosing them, to make them the common property of the nation . . . The press lives by disclosures.

It is not always easy to fulfill the responsibility. For several weeks in 1961, the world's important newsgathering organizations tried to get reporters into Portugal's African colony of Angola to cover the bloody fighting there, but Portugal wasn't giving any visas. On the other hand, since 1956 our own State Department has refused to permit American journalists to go to Red China; in continuing this refusal, the State Department has seemed to accept the underlying philosophy of the Communists— that journalists can be influenced by and are the tools of governments. It is the obligation of journalism to cover Red China; with freedom of the press curtailed by our own hand in this area, we have no idea of what some 669 million people are up to.

The obligations and responsibilities are many. They include covering the United Nations as thoroughly as Washington and your state capital are covered; but do the papers you read and the stations you watch and hear really cover it as they should? Does television live up to journalism's obligation to disclose "the most correct intelligence of the events of the time" during the evening hours when the greatest number of people are able to tune in—or does it offer sheer insulation from the realities of the world? The press has an obligation to look behind closed doors, to poke and pry; but does the press you know smoke things out—or does it wait for the news to happen? The press has a responsibility to educate (newspapers, by law, are delivered free of postal charge in the county where they are published, because they are educational materials), and a responsibility to endow its audience with a set of values. But not long ago the plane of a $30,000-a-year American mercenary pilot on an intelligence mission was shot down.

When the pilot fell into Russian hands he pleaded that he "never paid any attention to politics in America" and had "never voted." He was aware of neither the coming summit meeting in Paris nor of the implications of his flight. He seemed to have no values; he just flew for pay in a job which his President described as "vital to the defense of our country."

Then there is the obligation to take a stand: to editorialize. And it belongs as much to the local TV and radio station as it does to the *New York Times*. The responsibility to follow up a story is too seldom fulfilled; the pace of sensationalism seems to be such that one rarely finds out what happened afterward.

A couple of generations back, a journalist named Finley Peter Dunne said the duty of a newspaper was "to afflict the comfortable and comfort the afflicted." A journalist of the present generation named James Reston has said, "Power in any free society has to be watched. The greater the power, the greater the need for skepticism on the part of the press." Put these statements together and you have one of the most important obligations of the press: to be the watchdog of government. This role the press delights in. But while it enjoys afflicting the government, it seldom afflicts the comfortable any more in the way, for instance, that brought the word "muckraking" into the language. Rather, the crusades of today are those which comfort the afflicted. Crusading journalism comforts the public that is victimized by crime, the elderly in nursing homes, the migrant worker, the youngsters who are about to become dope addicts, the inmates of mental hospitals, the occupants of slums, the mass who hope to see the end of disease in their time.

## The Power of the Press

With its freedom, its rights, its obligations, hasn't the press in the American scheme of things a great deal of power?

It has and it hasn't. As you proceed in journalism, you will hear much talk from time to time of the power of the press. In practice, this is many kinds of power. The press not only has the right to inform and enlighten, it has the power to. In a democracy, every citizen has the right to access to information, to inform himself on how his elected officials are conducting his government. As "the fourth branch of government," the press serves a utilitarian purpose: It acts as censor of the government. This was recognized by Thomas Jefferson when he said, "No government ought to be without censors, and while the press is free, no one will."

Today this power is so strong that much of government is by press conference and trial balloon; publicity is as important to the government as taxes. For not only does the press recognize its role as the fourth branch—the government recognizes it, too. This power is valuable to individuals in the government—the late Secretary of State John Foster Dulles was a past master at the art of using the power of the press, and President Truman, who held press conferences more regularly than any other Chief Executive, said he learned a great deal from the reporters; and this power is corruptible by individuals in the government—the late Senator Joseph McCarthy had only one weapon, but he had it fully at his command: the weapon of publicity.

But more important is the press itself playing the role of censor of the government. And it is played at every level of government and in every corner of the country, from the Los Angeles papers fighting the starvation of the program for our only anti-missile missile, the Nike-Zeus, to the Denver papers exposing police scandals, to the New York papers censoring a re-elected mayor and his Board of Estimate for voting themselves raises and new Cadillacs —all of which adds up to the power of the press as civic conscience.

The power of advocacy is the kind that finds expression principally in editorials. It is a power little exercised these days for unpopular causes, but greatly used for those which are popular, both in the editorial columns and in feature stories. The principal area in which the press has traditionally exercised its power of advocacy is in political elections. The press gets all excited about which paper is backing whom; it was news in the other New York papers when the *Times* endorsed Lefkowitz against Wagner and when the *Daily News* remained neutral. When it ran the famous picture showing a hole in Adlai Stevenson's shoe, the press was accused of (1) trying to humanize the candidate; and (2) trying to injure him—depending on which side you were on. And despite the accusation that communication is controlled by a "one-party press" (i.e., Republican), the other party seems to win plenty of elections, too. The truth is that the press, with its power of advocacy, is more likely to jump onto a bandwagon than to start one rolling or take the reins.

Another power of the press is criticism. The press is our guide to good and bad in matters cultural: books, music, art, architecture, and drama. Seldom does a Broadway play survive the blasts of a handful of newspaper critics. The printed media do not hesitate to criticize the broadcast media (though why a "television critic" should reign over TV drama, music, opera, political broadcasts, sports, children's programs, or other special coverage when each of these is the area of a specialist in the newspaper's own columns, nobody knows). But the printed media are themselves highly sensitive to criticism.

Finally, the press has the power to protect. In reporting on government at every level, the journalist almost unconsciously magnifies the good qualities and minimizes the bad as he sees them in the public official. More than one President of the United States has enjoyed the protective power of the press. And then there is the absolute power of the press—the power that makes newspaper delivery trucks the only commercial vehicles permitted to use New York City parkways, the power that gains partial government subsidy for publications through special postal rates, the power that exempts newsboys from wage and hour laws.

Freedom and power—almost no other business in America enjoys so much of each. Therefore it is important for the aspiring journalist to recognize another responsibility of the press: the responsibility for self-discipline. It is up to the journalist himself to make sure that journalism does not abuse its freedom or its power. And it is up to the journalist to realize that he is as much a public servant as any elected official.

Public service is prominent among the duties of journalism. It ranges from the *New York Herald Tribune's* annual Fresh Air Fund, which sends thousands of children from city streets to country vacations each summer, to the *Philadelphia Inquirer's* court action to back up an editorial campaign to open the world-famous Barnes art collection (a tax-free foundation)to the public.

When the *New York Times* reproduces in its entirety the government's booklet on what to do about a nuclear attack, or when any newspaper sponsors free polio shots or swimming lessons for youngsters—that's public service. On television in 1961, about $320 million worth of free time was devoted to public service causes, with the average station contributing $153,249 worth in the third quarter of the year alone. Two peculiarities about TV public service programing: It is not unusual to see a Presidential press conference interrupted in the middle of one of the President's answers, followed by an invitation to "stay tuned for cartoon fun," and it is a fact of television life that an audience of ten million for a public service program is so small, by commercial TV standards, that the program may be broadcast at inconvenient hours, such as early Sunday morning.

News is big business. And anybody in business is there to make a profit. The major factor in the profit picture for any medium of news and information is advertising—and

no medium will find advertising revenue coming into its
till unless it "delivers" an audience of readers or viewers or
listeners that is the one to whom the advertiser sells his
goods. The reader of the newspaper or magazine pays part
of the cost of what he reads; the television or radio audience pays nothing directly for what it sees or hears in the
living room. TV and radio are subject to regulation as
to what percentage of their time is devoted to advertising,
whereas newspapers and magazines are subject neither to
regulation nor to limitation. And you will learn at your
first newspaper job that the business office tells the editor
how many columns are available for news.

At many newspapers, a favorable year-end balance is
achieved thanks only to the television station which the
paper owns and operates. But it is interesting to note that
the dozen or so newspapers that do best financially are just
about the same dozen or so considered best in quality when
surveys are taken. The *New York Times*, the *Christian
Science Monitor*, the *Wall Street Journal*, the *St. Louis
Post-Dispatch*, the *Milwaukee Journal*, the *Washington
Post*, the *Louisville Courier-Journal*, the *Chicago Tribune*,
the *Chicago Daily News*, the *Kansas City Star*, the *Los
Angeles Times*, the *New York Herald Tribune*—these are
the big boys, any way you look at them.

# THREE

## *The First Steps*

WHAT DOES IT TAKE to get started in journalism? If you like to find things out, if you like to know what's going on around you, if you like to talk with people and know how to listen, and if you know what to ask next, you are already on your way. You have already begun because talking and listening are still the best ways of finding things out. They are still the most important tools of the journalist. Another is the power of observation. You should practice using all three of these tools, developing your ability to get people to talk about the things you want to know, learning to remember what they say, improving your power to see things as they really are.

As a reporter, you will find that even idle conversation can turn up something you would like to know. Usually you will be seeking the right information from the right people. Your news sources may range from the operator of the filling station around the corner, if you are the editor of a small town weekly, to the number one man in the White House, if you happen to be a Washington correspondent. You will learn to respect each source equally.

*65*

What you report and write will be little better than your sources of information. The man at the filling station may not know anything about our foreign policy, but the man in the White House won't know when the mayor's car has been gassed up for a long trip, either.

### Imagination, Curiosity, and Judgment

The good reporter has a compulsion to get to the heart of things. This means he has imagination, too. Without it, he won't think of where to look or what to ask in his search for the facts, the truth, and the better story. When the governor of New York reported that Premier Khrushchev had told him he once nearly emigrated to America, one reporter put through a call to the Kremlin to check the story with the ultimate source. It didn't really matter that the Soviet leader wouldn't come to the phone. He might have.

What we have been talking about is curiosity. You should have plenty of it, plenty of leg power, and plenty of good judgment. With any kind of luck, all three will improve with experience, although the legs are bound to give out some day.

There is no point in setting out to be a hard-boiled guy. The really good reporter isn't made up that way. But he does have a job that requires him to try to put his emotions aside every now and then. This is something you will understand only after you have covered your first fatal plane crash or your first feature from a slum where the children who sleep together in one room are outnumbered only by the rats in the walls.

If you become a doctor, one of your most important
assets will be your selflessness. If you become a lawyer,
your ability to hunt down a precedent or convince a jury
will serve you well, but your respect for the law will deter-
mine what kind of lawyer you will be. Your mental outlook
is just as important in journalism. It is hard for a doctor
to go wrong as long as his patient's health is his first consideration, or for a lawyer if he attends always to the best
interests of his client. Both have professional standards
and rules of ethics to follow. In journalism, you will
usually have only your own attitude and your own judgment, good or bad, to guide you.

This is something you should realize from the beginning. There will be editors to tell you where to go, what
to cover, what to write, and what to rewrite. But editors
are little real help to reporters and writers in a lot of
ways.

If you are sent across town to cover a fire, it will be up
to you to find the battalion chief, the owner of the building,
the heroic fireman. You will have to describe the scene and
find out where the fire began, what caused it, how it spread,
and what the damage is.

If you are sitting up late at Ndola waiting for the arrival of the United Nations Secretary-General, it will be
up to you to decide whether to take the word of someone
else that he has landed.

If you are a member of the Washington press corps
attending a Presidential press conference, it will be up to
you whether to say to the President, "Sir, two well-known
security risks have recently been put on a task force in the

State Department to help reorganize the Office of Security."

If you are a columnist for the Associated Press, it will
be up to you whether to accept a free cruise to South
America from the builders of a new ship you have written
about.

These situations have all occurred. The people who faced
them decided for themselves what to do. At Ndola, the
word of someone else was taken, as reporters so often have
to do, when in fact the Secretary-General's plane had
already crashed. The Washington reporter did label two
men as security risks and the AP columnist had a whale
of a time on his cruise.

Much of today's news comes pre-gathered and pre-
written in the form of public relations handouts, leaving
the reporter or rewriteman little more to do than rewrite
the handout. Still, there will be many times when getting
the story will mean seeing your opportunities and seizing
them. In Washington, the best story of the day may come
from the President's quick answer to a question as he
escorts a visiting chief of state to his car, or from a casual
huddle with the President's press secretary late at night.

Telling the story, at least telling it well, is a matter of
good writing. News stories are written under the pressure
of their importance and under the pressure of the deadline.
If you have no knack at all for putting one word after
another, you will have a hard time in journalism. Even so,
you *can* learn to write well enough, no matter how little
writing ability you have to start with.

An essential ingredient of the straightforward news

story is its objectivity—a word that gives some of journalism's big thinkers a good bit of their intellectual exercise. They wonder whether anyone can be really objective. All that is really meant, and all that is required, is an honest effort to be impartial, to present both sides of an issue and not to judge.

## What Is News?

Well, you say, What *is* news? Shouldn't I be able to define it?

Perhaps you should, but definitions vary. News is what you find out today that you didn't know before. News is that which informs and enlightens the reader. News is what nobody sees coming—the collapse of a grandstand at Indianapolis, a snapped cable in the Alps, death beneath the high wire, a collision at sea. And it is what everybody has been waiting for—the end of a war, the election returns, the first American to orbit the earth, the birth of a boy to a princess.

Some is worth putting on the front page, or giving five minutes out of fifteen. Some will always end up on the dead hook or in the overset.

# FOUR

## *Qualifications and Goals*

HOW FAR CAN I GO? What do I need to get there? These two questions are uppermost in your mind as you consider any career.

In most businesses the pattern of growth and development in your career would be one of ever-increasing wages and ever-broadening responsibility, reaching toward a pinnacle of success as an executive—or even as president of a corporation. This has been likened to a pyramid of achievement: With a broad base of workers at the bottom, the pyramid grows smaller with each step toward the top, leaving room at each level for fewer of the experts. The better you are as an executive and administrator, guiding and developing the work of others, the higher you climb on the pyramid.

### The Pyramid of Achievement

Journalism has its pyramid of achievement—but with important differences, because journalism is much more than a business. Often a journalist finds himself so dedicated to what he is doing at one level on the pyramid that he is willing to forego the chance to make more money or to tell others what to do. And often he is simply a better journalist by not moving up. Since administration pays better than reporting, it may take some dedication to level off at what you like and do best.

The broad base of the pyramid of achievement is made up of those who are not basically trained for the field, either by education or experience. They might work just as well in any business; they happen to be in journalism. In this group you will find clerical workers: secretaries, stenographers, and the vast number of people who keep accounts straight. At *Time* magazine, if you count all employees from mail clerks and those in the subscription office through those who sell advertising space and handle promotions, only one out of seven works in an editorial capacity, gathering, writing, and editing news and information. Six out of seven, then, are in journalism but are basically untrained for it; they could perform the same function in another field. Among them, of course, there are always some who have the interest and dedication to move upward into the editorial area.

But those to whom this book is directed will be found on different levels of the pyramid. They are those who are trained by education and experience to gather and disseminate news and information.

With few exceptions, the young journalist today is college-educated. The question, then, is not whether to go to college but what kind of college to go to, and what courses to take.

*College Courses in Journalism*

There is a wide range of possibilities. At most Ivy
League colleges, you will be hard put to find the word
*journalism*, let alone a course in journalism, in the
catalogue. On the other hand, there are scores of colleges
and universities where the opportunity to major in journalism is offered. Of these, about fifty offer programs
which have won approval from the American Council on
Education for Journalism, the recognized accrediting
agency in the field. Certain colleges are well known for
their programs in journalism; if you say you went to
Missouri, one is likely to assume that you majored in
journalism. At Missouri you have the option of taking a
five-year program in journalism instead of the usual four-
year course. If you go to Medill, Northwestern's school
of journalism, you have no option: You spend five years.
The Columbia University School of Journalism is strictly
a one-year postgraduate course of study.

So all kinds of programs and courses in journalism are
available. What should you take? Should you major in
journalism, or in the broader liberal arts field and develop
your qualifications for journalism later, either in graduate work, as at Columbia, or on the job?

This is the classic problem for young people who are
interested in this field, and a classic difference of opinion
has long existed between the educators and the working
press. Believe it or not, there are still some old-timers who
prefer to hire young people at eighteen and train them

on the job—without benefit of higher education. Fortunately, those with this viewpoint are now rare. But there are enough who are dead set against teaching journalism in the classroom that it must be noted. Only a few years ago Mark Ethridge, publisher of the *Louisville Courier-Journal* and the *Louisville Times*, said:

> I may have been entirely wrong, but I have told my own children in years past not to take journalism as an undergraduate course; that the best they could get out of it was a short-cut in techniques; that it was more important to fill their minds than to learn a trade. Schools of journalism have improved vastly since I gave that advice, but it is still basically true. I should like to see the schools recast so that the techniques of journalism become incidental, or at least could be learned as extra-curricular activity, while the emphasis is put upon making the full man intellectually, and upon learning more of what to write than how to write the five W's. My ideal school of journalism would be heavy in English and English Literature (I might even require Latin); in history of every kind including archaeology; in political science and in economics.

The direction Mr. Ethridge describes is the direction the better journalism schools have been taking. At the accredited schools, the typical student now spends only about 20 to 25 percent of his classroom work in journalism courses, with the majority of his time devoted to the basic disciplines of a liberal education. English literature, the humanities and behavioral sciences, history and politics and economics, one or two of the sciences and certainly one or two languages—these are the courses for the so-called journalism major. Furthermore, in most programs today, courses in specific areas of journalism are offered only in the upper-class years.

By the same token, at most of the accredited schools the emphasis is more upon the theories and philosophies of journalism than upon its techniques. More important than learning the difference between letterpress and offset printing, or between Bodoni and Cheltenham typefaces, or between voice-over and on-camera, is learning to discriminate between the important and the unimportant, the ethical and the unethical, the responsible and the irresponsible. Learning *why* ideas are communicated is more important than learning what the machines do.

And in almost any of the colleges that offer accredited journalism programs, you will have ample opportunity to practice techniques in extracurricular activities on the campus newspaper and broadcasting stations. In some instances, this means more than just campus publications. At Missouri, the student publication, the *Columbia Missourian,* is the daily and Sunday newspaper of general circulation for the city of Columbia and Boone County.

Columbia University, Missouri, Medill—these schools command the respect even of the diehards who consider "trade schools" in the field a waste of time. But if the "trade school" image of journalism schools is dying hard among editors and publishers, it may be because some who sustain the image have been too busy in recent years to look at the accredited schools or their graduates. Presently underrated is the extent to which journalism *is* a liberal art, the extent to which journalism students in recent years have acquired a set of values of their own, the extent to which they have developed an interest in what is happening in the world and learned how to express themselves.

## Journalism Supermarkets

Now, just a word about the journalism school to watch out for. There are many, in colleges all around the country, that are not accredited by the American Council on Education for Journalism. These are journalism supermarkets, offering a broad range of technical or "trade school" courses in preparation for jobs in the media and advertising end of the business. If you are dedicated to spending a lifetime in the gathering and dissemination of news and information, a journalism major at such a college will stand you in poorer stead than the solid general college education with a side order of journalism which you will get in your journalism major at an accredited school. (See Appendix A for a list of journalism programs currently accredited by the ACEJ.)

## Schools of Journalism vs. Courses

With few exceptions, schools of journalism are regional in character and orientation; that is, they draw from nearby counties and states for their students, and their graduates usually head for jobs in the same general area. Deans and directors of placement keep in close touch with state and regional editors and publishers, who look to them to provide new recruits each year and who help support many of the colleges with financial contributions.

The exceptions? Again, Columbia, Medill, Missouri, and perhaps four or five others, which may be considered national in scope and character because they draw from all over the country and even from other parts of the world.

Journalism turns up in the college curriculum in another form, too. Some colleges and universities do not have a school or department of journalism. Instead, they integrate journalism with other courses. Professor Edgar E. Folk, of Wake Forest College, describes it this way:

> The student takes a major in English or the Social Sciences, with a minor in the other. The journalism courses, which are in the English Department, are taken as electives and are conducted probably more as liberal arts courses than vocational courses. We try to make them broadly educational. For instance, the text book in the course in newswriting is a subscription to *The New York Times*. We feel that a student should learn by his daily reading of that what news is and how it is handled; he should also learn how to read a paper and should acquire the habit of keeping up with some of today's drama. Of course, he does a good deal of writing of various sorts of stories. We think that our duty is to weed out quickly all students who have no distinct aptitudes for newspaper work. The time spent in learning what *The Times* is and how to read it will not hurt even these.

## Graduate Study and Fellowships

Columbia offers the master's degree to those who have had little or no undergraduate journalism training and intend to earn their living as practicing newsmen. Medill's fifth year brings with it the master's degree, but the

Medill student has been getting his feet wet in journalism courses during his four earlier years at Northwestern. At other universities, work for the master's degree will take you more toward research and teaching than practice, or will give you specialization (Wisconsin, for instance, offers a graduate program which works closely with its specialized Department of Agricultural Journalism). You can go for a Ph.D. in journalism, too—but chances are that will mean you are committed to teaching and research. You will find few managing editors ready to move over and give up their jobs to someone because he has a Ph.D.

Some journalists go back to school after several years on the job. The foremost programs for experienced newsmen are the Nieman fellowships at Harvard and the American Press Institute at Columbia.

The Nieman fellowships provide a year's study in the journalist's special field of interest; the science reporter or editor may spend his year in science courses, the court reporter may take courses in the Harvard Law School, and so on. Applicants must have at least three years' practical experience and be currently employed by a newspaper or wire service.

The American Press Institute consists of two-week seminars covering all phases of newspaper operations, and it brings together several groups of experts—managing editors for one seminar, picture editors for another, advertising managers for a third, and so on—with the purpose of contributing to the improvement of newspapers by the seminar method of analysis and critique. The API requires five years' experience on a daily newspaper, with participants nominated and sponsored by their newspaper management.

Neither the Nieman program nor the API demands formal education requirements and no course credits or degrees are awarded by either. Neither broadcast nor magazine journalists are eligible.

Other programs and fellowships include the King Fellowships in Journalism at the University of Colorado, a five-week "Little Nieman" plan; a new advanced international reporting program, supported by the Ford Foundation, at Columbia; the CBS Foundation News fellowships, for representatives of broadcast journalism, and the Rockefeller fellowships in science writing at Columbia; and the Newspaper Fund's fellowships for high school and college journalism teachers or advisers who wish to improve their knowledge of journalism. Then there are many undergraduate scholarships and grants, from the Inter-American Press Association Scholarship Fund, awarding eight $2,500 scholarships annually, to the William Randolph Hearst Foundation, which has awarded as much as $40,900 a year in fellowships.

Independent graduate work is not unusual, either. More than one journalist has put himself through night law school in order to improve his reporting ability in court and government work. Others have studied science, economics, and political science.

Does formal education automatically mean a place higher up on the pyramid of achievement? Not necessarily. Unlike teaching or medicine or the science of physics, there seems to be no real correlation between higher education and higher position in journalism.

*Prizes and Awards*

There are certain prizes and awards which bring high honor to the journalist. Foremost among these are the Pulitzer prizes, established in 1903 and first awarded in 1917 as part of the School of Journalism which Joseph Pulitzer, then publisher of the *St. Louis Post-Dispatch* and the *New York World*, gave to Columbia University. These prizes consist of a gold medal award to a newspaper for outstanding public service and of seven other prizes of $1,000 each to individuals—two in local reporting, and one each in national reporting, international reporting, editorial writing, editorial cartooning, and photography. (Pulitzer prizes are also awarded in letters, drama, and music.) In 1962, the jurors went through some seven hundred journalism entries, many of them such large presentations that limitations on the size of entries have since been imposed.

The Ayer Cup awards go to newspapers for fine work in typography, makeup, and printing, and to stimulate interest in improving the appearance and readability of newspapers. For individuals, the Maria Moors Cabot awards recognize journalistic achievements which advance international friendship in the Western Hemisphere. The University of Missouri recognizes broadcast journalists as well as the traditional press in making its honor awards for distinguished service in journalism during its annual Journalism Week. Sigma Delta Chi, the national journalism society, awards perhaps the greatest number of separate prizes. Among dozens more, the prizes most coveted by newsmen are the Mike Berger awards for news writing, the Heywood Broun Award for outstanding journalistic achievement, and the George Foster Peabody awards for achievement in news (among several categories) in radio and TV.

Sometimes a little enterprise will go a long way and win a prize. The annual Byline Award of the New York Newspaper Reporters Association for 1961 went to a reporter who did no more than he had been assigned to do. That was to report what happened at a luncheon. The luncheon, however, was one at which New York builders and real estate men—a number of whom did business with the city— were called upon to announce how much they would contribute to the mayor's campaign for re-election.

"Although other reporters were at the luncheon," the reporter's paper said in its story of the award, its man had "recognized the significance of the affair. He rushed to phone his office, still adding up the pledges that had been announced . . . Because it was by then after 2 P.M., [his] call was given to a rewriteman, a practice used by newspapers to speed publication of late-breaking stories. The rewriteman . . . got the facts . . . and wrote the story rapidly enough for it to appear in the last three editions . . ." (*New York World-Telegram and Sun*, April 16, 1962.)

## The Testing Ground

Where and how can you test your interest in the field? You can test it wherever you are, and in many ways.

One place is your high school or college paper or yearbook. Deadlines are little different from the ones you will face later. Covering a speech on campus poses the same problems in getting the story as covering a speech in Convention Hall or Madison Square Garden—and perhaps more, since the campus speaker may not provide a text ahead of time. Reporting high school sports requires the same knowledge of the game and as good observation of the contest as reporting the major leagues.

If you have established an interest by working on a student paper, you may get a chance to breathe the air of journalism more deeply by participating in such affairs as New York University's Workshop for High School Editors or the Scholastic Press Association meetings at Columbia. Three- and four-day sessions offer speeches, seminars, and contests. Each year the best high school journalists from every state in the Union come to the Medill School of Journalism. Between junior and senior years they meet for five weeks of specialized study in "Journalism and the World of Ideas."

In twelve states, the Future Journalists of America operates at the high school level, under the wing of Sigma Delta Chi and Theta Sigma Phi, the national society for women in journalism. Quill and Scroll is the international honorary society for high school journalists, with charters in eight thousand American high schools. It sets standards for school papers, yearbooks, and magazines, and sponsors contests and recommends other activities.

If you are in high school, your guidance adviser can tell you which of these or other organizations is active where you are. Take advantage of them to test your interest now. When two groups of college editors and

graduate journalism students were surveyed not long ago,
nearly half said they had made up their minds to go into
journalism before they had left high school.

Opportunities to test your interest are even greater
while you are in college. You can work as a campus stringer
for the local paper in the town where you go to college or
for your hometown paper. As Simmons Fentress, editorial
writer for the *Charlotte Observer* says, "A stint on a
campus paper can tell an aspiring journalist—usually
but not always—whether he really has printer's ink in his
veins or whether he should take Pop's advice and come
back home to run the lard factory." ("The Newspaper
Job," *Nieman Reports*, April 1958.) Some local radio
stations man their sports departments year in, year out,
with part-time help from nearby campuses. A part-time
job during semesters often develops into a full-time job
during the summer, when papers and stations need inex-
pensive replacements for people on vacation. You can
even be a stringer for a free-lance journalist: One member
of the Society of Magazine Writers keeps a list of thirty
students and part-time journalists around the country on
whom he can call for help in interviewing or digging up
information in their areas.

On some college campuses, you will find that nearby
newspapers regularly send editors to conduct student
workshops, seminars, or clinics. Sit in on these whenever
you can, to increase your knowledge and to test your
interest. And then look for chances to go from the campus
to the newspaper. The best testing ground is the *summer
internship*, which gives you a chance to work in the daily

newspaper operation. A fair number of papers provide
summer internships. Some offer the same pay you would
have starting as a regular employee. Some, in effect, are
scholarships or fellowships with stipends provided by the
college or some other sponsor. Some reward the student
with course credits upon completion of satisfactory work.
Some of the best are offered by the *St. Petersburg Times*,
in Florida, and the *Des Moines Register and Tribune*,
which goes so far as to bring Dr. William E. Hall, director
of the University of Nebraska school of journalism, to a
regular job on the *Register* copy desk and to the chair-
manship of weekly seminars for the interns. "By inference
and illustration," says Dr. Hall, "the interns learned that
expert craftsmanship in journalism is not the mastering of
mechanical skills but the end result of a complicated and
continuing thought-evaluation-judgment process." The
*Minneapolis Star and Tribune* takes some interns, too.
The University of Michigan places about twenty-five of
its undergraduates and graduate students in journalism on
newspapers around the country for the summer. Time
Inc. offers summer jobs in New York to college students,
but without an internship program or any formal training; could there be a better way to look around inside
the field of magazine journalism? The Gannett newspapers, in Rochester, New York, take aspiring journalists
into a thirteen-week training program. At Missouri, even
after you have signed up as a journalism major, you can
test your appetite further during summers and holiday
periods by working full time on the *Missourian*. The City
News Bureau in Chicago has an internship program for

graduate students at Medill, providing six credit hours for the course, plus pay at the bureau's regular rates. The news department of the American Broadcasting Company in New York regularly employs one journalism student each from Columbia and the Annenberg School of the University of Pennsylvania.

The Newspaper Fund, supported by grants from the *Wall Street Journal,* in recent years has helped find summer jobs for students in colleges where there is little recruiting for newspaper careers. In 1961, 141 students were placed in newsrooms of 108 newspapers in 28 states, and, upon successful completion of the summer's work, each was awarded a $500 scholarship toward his next year's college expenses. These are by no means all the opportunities. Any one of them, whether officially an internship, with a formal training program, or simply a summer job, will have three important benefits beyond testing your interest. First, it will enhance the value of your later college courses. When you return to theories and classrooms in the fall, you will have practical experience to guide you. Second, you will be able to move into your first regular job with greater confidence. Third, you may be able to command higher starting pay.

Watch for the activities of press clubs where you are. State, regional, and city-wide press associations sponsor conventions, speeches, clinics. National Newspaper Week is celebrated every October. Attend whatever you can, so that you can get the feel of the business and get to know people in it.

High school journalism isn't always easy. When New

York City teachers went on strike for two days, there was some violence at one school and a *Herald Tribune* photographer took a picture of one student being hauled away by a policeman. The caption? "At right, Martin Lewis, photographer of the Taft Yearbook, is 'escorted' to school by policeman after he was told not to take pictures of the egg-throwing incident and its aftermath."

If the police did not know that Martin Lewis was on the tough testing ground of journalism that day, at least one Brooklyn reader did. Ronald S. Mintz, in a letter to the editor which the *Tribune* published a few days later, said, "What right has the local government to even tell a photographer not to record events occurring in the public streets? If the police prohibit people from photographing news events, there is no freedom of the press." (The *New York Herald Tribune*, April 26, 1962.)

# FIVE

## *Reporting and Rewriting*

GETTING THE STORY is only half the job. It must also be told. But the individual who gets the story is not always the one who tells it. That is, the reporter doesn't always write the story and, when he does, it is often told all over again by a rewriteman.

Because the reporter is "the shock trooper of the entire operation" and his work "the foundation of all journalism" (Simmons Fentress, "The Newspaper Job," *Nieman Reports,* April 1958) this chapter will go into some detail about him and about the rewriteman. They are the ones who get the story and put it on paper. The next chapter will discuss the editor, because he is the one who decides what use is to be made of the story, which stories are to be covered, how they are covered, and how much time or space can be devoted to the story.

### Getting the Story

Like any other writer, the reporter begins not by putting words to paper but by getting the story. This is the plain physical legwork. The distance may be across the city room to the newspaper library or "morgue" or across the city, state, or country. Digging out facts calls for painstaking investigation and research, carefully handled interviews, plus a shrewd combination of conjecture, hunch, and luck. And the reporter's task is a learning task. Olive Ewing Clapper, widow of the late columnist Raymond Clapper, has provided a fine description of the task:

> First and foremost, it was hard work, working hard every day, eating up important information, digesting it, writing it, always adhering to his own instinctive integrity—that's terribly important—applying the seat of his pants to the seat of the chair with the hands on the typewriter and reading and studying and then asking the right questions. (*One Lucky Woman*. Garden City, N. Y.: Doubleday & Company, Inc., 1961.)

Asking the right questions is vitally important to getting the story and getting it right. What the journalist doesn't know or hasn't found in the public relations handout, or in the library, may be learned from others closer to the subject. There are always questions that only an expert can answer—but he can answer them only if they are asked. So the reporter must know whom to ask and what to ask. The reporter who interviews only the minister who sponsored a jazz mass will not write half as good a story as the reporter who thinks, "There must be some people in the congregation who don't approve of this," and also finds and interviews the outraged parishioner.

The good reporter works his powers of observation to the bone, seeing details that ordinary folk overlook. He

can look into a stranger's face and know whether the
answers he is getting are the truth or a partial truth and
whether something is being held back. And he sees details
which will make his story the only authentic account.

Notice how a reporter's eye for detail helped this
story of a Presidential visit to a Coast Guard training
bark:

WASHINGTON, Aug. 15 — A
sailor President went down to the
Navy Yard Annex on Anacostia
River this morning to review a
noble sailing ship—the Coast
Guard's training bark, *Eagle.*

The three-masted vessel, carrying 160 cadets, stopped in Washington on its way back to the
Coast Guard Academy at New
London, Conn., after a summer
cruise to European ports. The
cadets were all first- and third-
year men.

In preparation for the inspec-
tion, her white paint had been
scrubbed, the oak deck holystoned
and the brass heads of the belay-
ing pins polished.

Just before the President arrived, 100 cadets scrambled up
the ratlines and manned the yard
arms of the fore and main masts,
and the lines of the gaff topsail
and spanker on the mizzen mast.

The President was piped
aboard, stood at attention amid-
ships while "Hail to the Chief"

was played, inspected the honor
guard, cast his eye over the rig-
ging dotted with the white-clad
cadets and said:

"Magnificent!"

Then the third-year men came
down the ratlines while the first-
year men exercised their privilege
of sliding down the backstays to
the deck. E. W. Kenworthy, the
*New York Times*, August 16,
1962. (Copyright *The New York
Times*. Used by permission.)

The reporter usually is on his own, dependent on his
own resources. He develops his own shorthand, his own
filing system, his own way of interviewing.

His tools are few and simple. Pen or pencil, folded
copypaper or pad, typewriter, telephone (and dimes in
pocket), dead hook, paper cutter, scissors, paste pot,
microphone stick, tape recorder, and camera (still or
motion picture).

While the reporter is a "loner" on many assignments,
and almost always in outlook, he is often thrown together
with other reporters when big news breaks. When Khrushchev visited Iowa, packs of reporters trampled whole
fields of corn. When Eddie Fisher broke with Liz Taylor,
reporters thronged the corridors of a New York hotel
seventy strong. When New York's first "Barnes dance,"
a new system of traffic lights, was held, more reporters than
pedestrians jammed the sidewalk. At such times, reporters
often work together as best they can to get the story, interviewing together and comparing notes.

Some of the difficulties encountered in getting the story are shown in an incident that occurred when the Republic of the Congo's public relations firm arranged what was to have been an exclusive interview between Congo Premier Cyrille Adoula and a woman television reporter. Just prior to the interview, Soviet UN delegate Zorin visited the African leader and, departing, encountered a crowd of reporters and photographers who wanted to know how the visit had gone. Carefully evading questions about what he had discussed with the African leader, Mr. Zorin boarded the elevator. Immediately Mr. Adoula stepped from his suite for the interview with the television reporter. An American press agent, fluent in French, served as interpreter while the TV reporter asked about the Congo and the UN but nothing about Mr. Zorin's unexpected visit. At last she did ask what the African and Russian had discussed. The premier replied that Mr. Zorin had given him an explanation of the attitude the Soviet Union had expressed toward the Congo in the United Nations a few days before.

The reporter said into the microphone, "Thank you very much, Cyrille Adoula, premier of the Congo," and the interview was over. As the interpreter slipped quietly out the door, the rest of the reporters tried to find out *what* the "explanation" had been. But the premier spoke no English. The reporters spoke no French. The press agent, having completed the exclusive interview to which Mr. Adoula had consented, had departed. A pack of reporters failed to get the essential fact of a story.

## Telling the Story

Having obtained the story, or as much of it as he can, the reporter puts it into a form in which the public will see or hear it. Whatever his medium, this is a writing job of some kind. It may be 300 to 600 words for a daily newspaper or a wire service. It may be a 1,500-word feature for the Sunday magazine section. It may be the 60-page script for a half-hour documentary or "white paper" on television or the one-page script for a 50-second segment of the six o'clock news. It may be a summary of events which transpired over a period of several days, written for a news magazine.

From the material at hand, the reporter tells his story so that the most hurried reader who scans the first paragraph, or listener who is paying only partial attention, will get the gist of it. Yet the story must give the thorough reader and careful listener every detail that can possibly be included. This calls for writing that is clear and crisp and simple: Plain good English, uncomplicated by involved sentence structure and uncluttered by flowery phrases. With style and syntax seemingly out of date, with even the latest dictionaries failing to take a firm stand about our language, it cannot be emphasized too strongly that clear writing is the key to good journalism. And with the great volume of writing a reporter turns out, this is not always easy. Under the grind of daily assignments and the pressure of the deadline, the most brilliant reporter or news writer can hardly be expected to turn out a brilliant piece of writing every time he puts paper into the type-writer.

Good newspaper writing is purposeful writing of three types: factual, interpretive, and opinion.

The factual report is journalism's traditional form. The old "who, what, when, where, and why" school of journalism simply gave the reader the facts and left him on his own to figure out what it was all about. This is writing that describes. It presents the information. Interpretive writing gives meaning to the facts. It may run from describing the setting or background of the event to explaining the sequences of happenings or to pointing out the significance of the story. A news story about a school bus that was hit by a train is factual when it tells all the details of the accident. It supplies an important piece of background when it points out how many similar accidents have occurred at the same crossing.

When the Russian premier bangs his shoe on his desk at the UN, you may be sure that most of those who write about it will offer interpretations of why he did it. In fact, almost all writing in journalism today is to some extent interpretive. Not all of it contains the explanatory box, "News Analysis," in the corner of the column. And not all of it needs to—for in this complicated world of news and information, a certain amount of interpretation helps the writing toward clarity and objectivity. It is the journalist's job not only to give the reader the facts, but to relate them to his experience and to past events, for it is the journalist's job to make the news understandable.

Opinion is another matter. The personal opinion of the journalist should be kept out of any news story, and so should the opinion of his employer. The story on the accident should not express the paper's or the broadcasting station's or the writer's opinion that the engineer or the bus driver was at fault. The UN correspondent should not express his opinion on what we should do about the man who bangs his shoe on the desk. Editorial writers are paid to express these opinions in the proper columns.

But drawing a line between interpretive writing and opinion isn't easy. CBS news analyst Howard K. Smith was considered by his employer to have carried analysis and interpretation of the news into the area of personal opinion. As a result, Smith and CBS terminated their relationship, and Smith was promptly hired by the ambitious ABC network, which announced that he would "speak his mind freely" and "do more than just report the news. He will explore its fundamental why's and how's— to arrive at the meaning of events. He will also state his own conclusions whenever he feels the facts warrant them." (Advertisement in *Saturday Review*, February 17, 1962, p. 7.)

Writing the story doesn't always mean that the reporter sits down at a typewriter. Often he rushes to the nearest telephone to dictate his story to a rewriteman back at the office. Frequently he selects his lead and composes it mentally while on the run, then dictates from the notes in his hand. Or, if he is in the broadcasting end of the business, he describes a situation or event while on the air or into a tape recorder—perhaps with a film or TV

camera observing him all the while—and has no chance to
see his words on paper or have them read back to him.

*Reporters' Assignments*

The reporter who phones in his story may be on *general
assignment*, or he may be a *district* or *beat* reporter.

The general assignment reporter is sent out from the
city room or newsroom each day, and no two days are
likely to bring the same kind of story to cover. He may
cover a hard news story, such as a fire or crime. He may
cover speeches or conferences or labor negotiations or other
predictable events such as building dedications or political
elections. He may cover visiting dignitaries on their sight-
seeing and ceremonial excursions.

The general assignment reporter must be equipped
with a wide frame of reference and general information.
He should know his city like the back of his hand and be
adept at such things as where to park his car in a hurry or
how to use the rapid transit system. The more sources he
has cultivated personally—policemen, firemen, neighborhood characters who know everything—as well as the more
prominent citizenry—the better he can cover whatever
story comes up. Often the foreign correspondent is really a
general assignment man in the city where he is stationed,
covering a political story one day, a financial story the
next, a story about labor or education or the arts on
another. Even today, general assignment can still mean
"the world is your beat." Within a few months, Homer
Bigart of the *New York Times* went from local news in
New York City, to New Guinea on the hunt for Michael

Rockefeller, to Israel for the judgment in the Adolf Eichmann trial, to South Vietnam to cover the guerrilla warfare there.

In a way, the district or beat man is an ancestor of today's special reporters and writers. The beat may be a police precinct, police headquarters, City Hall, or a courthouse. Other beats have been the waterfront, the garment district (in New York) and the ball park.

## *The Broadcast Reporter*

The broadcast reporter works in either of two ways: Using the special tools of his trade, he captures the story's immediacy and lets it be heard or heard and seen directly by his audience, or he writes the story for delivery as a summary or report to his audience. In the first instance, he films or videotapes the event or (in "live" coverage, as a ball game or space shot) lets it happen before his audience's eyes. This is expensive. Besides the reporter, it calls for at least a cameraman and sound engineer, plus lights if you're indoors, and a truck to carry all the equipment, and frequently it calls for a much larger crew.

Because time is money in broadcasting, this reporter must get something dramatic on the air in the shortest possible time—a minute or less, perhaps. And heavy expense combines with limited time to produce something that other reporters are slow to forgive. First, broadcast reporters have a way of not developing the interview, not framing the thoughtful, intelligent question, but of jumping in quickly with a short and often vague question that may provoke a brief but sufficiently interesting answer, as in the classic, "Would you say this is a pretty serious situation, Mr. Commissioner?" Second, because it is difficult and expensive to trundle all his equipment out to the hearing or the meeting, the broadcast reporter frequently tries to get in extra questions once he has arrived. While he has the mayor buttonholed before camera and microphone, he may try to pick up a good quote on a subject unrelated to the moment—for use in another current story, perhaps.

Stories which are not important enough to merit the attention of a crew on the scene still must be covered. Here, just as in the case of newspapers and wire services, the reporter goes out to get the story. He may phone it in to a rewriteman, or he may return to write it up himself. The writing is different from that for other media in a couple of respects. If it is for television, it must include some description or direction concerning what is to be shown while the story is told. Film clips from the station or network's reference files (somewhat similar to a newspaper's photo files or morgue) may be used. Some film or tape especially prepared for this report may be included. Charts, maps, or diagrams may be referred to. Or the reporter may simply be seen speaking to his audience. Whichever is used, clear and concise visual directions must be a part of the script.

Another significant difference in this kind of writing is that it is to be heard, not read. Words or phrases that have double meanings or cannot be easily understood when heard are to be avoided. What is heard should relate logically to what is being seen. The limitations of the clock are more demanding in some ways than those of the newspaper column. Most stories must be covered in a five or ten minute newscast and the total number of different stories may not be more than appear on only the front page of a daily newspaper.

Finally, in the newsroom, the broadcast reporter must be capable of making quick decisions and of organizing the station's resources when hard news breaks. A plane crash, a general-alarm fire, a tornado, call for bulletins on the air almost instantly, followed by decisions on coverage —how many men to send where, with what equipment. If you are the reporter who is on the desk when the news breaks, you have no time to stop and contemplate. You have to know what it will cost to send out a crew to cover the event, and whether its news value makes it worth it. You have to know whether to hold the story for the next newscast or interrupt whatever is on the air. If you can boast an average elapsed time of ninety seconds between learning of a bulletin story and reporting it to your listening audience, as NBC News currently boasts, you will be well out in front of your competitors.

There are places where the man who gets the story almost never writes it. At Time Inc., the system is known as "group journalism." Reporters and correspondents all over the world send reports to the headquarters of each Luce magazine, and a large number of researchers dig up more material, from all of which the staff in New York writes the final piece. At least one newspaper, the *Wall Street Journal*, operates this way to some extent. No matter where the dateline, many of the front page stories are written in New York. They call it "team journalism."

And *U. S. News & World Report* has been known to ascribe eyewitness stories to a "board of editors."

All of which brings up the question of credit and recognition for the reporter. The sight of one's own name at the top of a column of newsprint is a very special satisfaction; some reporters would rather have a byline than a raise. But the news magazines generally confer no bylines. Instead, they list staff members in the masthead. In the metropolitan press and the wire services, a byline today guarantees nothing more than that *somebody's* name has been placed at the top of the story. New York reporters have seen stories under their names on their days off. Bylines may be given to rewritemen who rewrote a story from a newspaper, or who took it over the phone from a reporter on the scene. A wire service story may appear verbatim in a newspaper with the name of one of the paper's reporters at the top. A double byline usually means that a reporter and a rewriteman have both been credited. When several writers and editors work on a story, the byline goes to the man who, in the editor's opinion, contributed the most.

### Rewrite

The rewriteman boils things down, reorganizes, and assembles. He recasts a wire story in the style of his paper or magazine or station. He constructs a comprehensive story from several reports from men on the scene. He has an automatic clock or column rule in his head, making a story come out to prescribed measure in an uncanny way. He is a careful listener when he takes a story over the phone, and he has the imagination to visualize the situation which is being described.

Rewrite is an inside job. If you like to get out and do the legwork, digging for a story, interviewing, seeing things for yourself, rewrite will not be for you. But if you thrive on deadline pressure, if speed at the typewriter is one of your big assets, and if you can organize material quickly, rewrite may be for you.

When a story is phoned in, the caller may be a reporter who left the office only an hour before, who has gathered details at the scene and is reporting from a phone booth. Or he may be a stringer in a small town fifty miles away who turns up with a story only once or twice a week. In any case, an important element in the rewriteman's work is collaboration with this caller. The better he knows his man, the better he can write the story.

If he's taking the story from a reporter or district man with whom he has daily contact and whose habits he knows pretty well, he can fill in much detail almost by intuition. If he's taking it from a stringer who is not too practiced a hand, he can wring extra details from him and probe for facts which the stringer might not have considered important. From hearing details over the phone, the rewriteman can gauge the importance of the story and whether it has been adequately covered by the man on the scene. Then he turns to, and in the shortest possible time writes it up.

As for rewriting, there are several kinds. We have mentioned that sometimes the reporter on the scene dictates sentence by sentence. Since the rewriteman is the only one

of the two who sees this dictation on paper, he may have
to touch it up or rewrite it entirely. Rewritemen spend
more time rewriting the handouts which pour in daily.
Seventy-five per cent of the material in *Time* and *Newsweek* is rewritten from the pages of the *New York Times*,
according to one estimate. Afternoon papers rewrite from
morning papers and morning papers rewrite from yesterday afternoon's papers. Broadcasters rewrite from newspapers, newspapers and broadcasters rewrite from wire
services, and wire services rewrite newspapers and themselves. New York offices rewrite copy from their overseas
operations.

There are some dangers inherent in the rewrite system.
Rewrite men frequently write on the basis of assumption,
and sometimes overlook the fact that changing one word
can change meaning. When *New York Times* reporter
Homer Bigart reported from Vietnam that U. S. helicopter
forces were being denied the Purple Heart medal, he described a man being "wounded in Communist fire" by metal
splinters from a seat bracket hit by a bullet. Next day, in
a story reporting that the President had authorized the
award of Purple Hearts to these men, the *Times* referred
to their having been "wounded by Communist fire." So a
delicate meaning, made precise by a careful reporter, was
undone by use of a different preposition.

Much of what the reporter and rewriteman do is routine news, routinely reported. John Hohenberg, professor
of journalism at Columbia and secretary of the Advisory
Board on Pulitzer prizes, describes some of the less routine:

What kind of stories are young people covering today, for which they win Pulitzer Prizes? Listen to these:

Mary Lou Werner, *Washington Evening Star,* in 1959 covered the school integration crisis in northern Virginia, dictating most of her stories by telephone on edition deadlines and exceeding her competition both in speed and accuracy and general interest.

Jack Nelson of the *Atlanta Constitution* in 1960 investigated the decline in efficiency of mental hospitals in the State of Georgia and obtained remedial action from the Legislature.

A. M. Rosenthal of the *New York Times,* covering for his newspaper behind the Iron Curtain, was thrown out of Poland by the Communist regime there, not because he didn't tell the truth, but because he probed too deeply into Communist affairs.

Edgar May, of the *Buffalo Evening News,* disclosed the shortcomings of the New York State program of relief for needy persons with such skill and sympathy that he won the thanks of the state Department of Welfare.

Sanche de Gramont of the *New York Herald Tribune* reported the death of baritone Leonard Warren on the stage of the Metropolitan Opera House with such effectiveness and speed on edition deadline that his work outshone all his distinguished competitors.

Here are the young journalists of today, covering stories and winning prizes in fields far different from the sensational crimes that preoccupied so many of my generation. That is the measure of the progress and the sophistication both of the reading public and of the journalist, as well. ("The Pulitzer Prizes and the American Press," remarks before the Columbia Scholastic Press Association of Columbia University, March 16, 1962.)

Besides such significant items, great human interest stories still break when you least expect them. Once in a while a real gem comes along, and a reporter and rewriteman know how to make the most of it. A good example is the Gallo story on the opposite page, from the *New York Daily News* of February 1, 1962.

# 7 of the Gallo Mob Rub Out Fire, Save Six

By JOSEPH KIERNAN and HENRY LEE

To the amazement of all South Brooklyn, especially themselves, the Gallo mob, generally considered the hillbilly hoodlums of the borough, were cast yesterday in a strange, blinding, new light.

As heroes.

Seven of them, headed by Larry Gallo, their temporary leader, bravely dashed through smoke and flame to rescue six small children from a third-floor apartment fire.

Larry, acting boss since the mob was left fatherless by the imprisonment of Crazy Joe Gallo, swallowed so much smoke in his moment of heroism that he required medical treatment. His six companions escaped, singed but safe, the terrific heat failing to explode even one of their cartridges.

### "We're Not Heroes"

Nonetheless, with the modesty of true heroes, though a fire battalion chief gave them unreserved commendation and the children's mother overwhelmed them with her gratitude, the hoods discounted their own bravery.

"Don't try to make heroes out of us," insisted Albert (Kid Blast) Gallo. "We're not heroes.

"We only done what any red-blooded American boys would do."

Kid Blast removed his hat and pointed at his head.

"Do you see any horns there?" he said plaintively. "I got no horns. We're not animals."

His voice lowered, and he added, "We're just human beings trying to get along."

### Just Having a Bite

The Gallos' giddy flirtation with valor occurred at 12:30 P.M. as the seven emerged from a luncheonette at 77 President St. to return to their heavily-guarded fortress nearby at 51 President St.

Usually, when the mob walks the block between Columbia and Van Brunt Sts., there are sudden popping noises from some passing car which the neighborhood stubbornly insists on calling backfire.

Yesterday's excitement, however, was a cloud of heavy smoke pouring out of a third-floor window at 73 President St., occupied by Mrs. Sista Biaz, 30. She had just gone to a grocery, leaving her six children, aged 10 months

**Larry Gallo**
*Just call me Chief*

to 6 years, alone in the four-room apartment.

"Come on!" yelled Larry.

Kid Blast took off after him. Following were Frank (Punchy) Illiano, Anthony Abbatemarco, Alphonse Serantonio, Leonard Dello and John Commarato.

The seven stomped up the stairs, broke into the smoke-filled apartment and found 5-year-old Evelyn Biaz with her hair afire.

One of the mob stripped off his jacket and smothered the flames.

Then they gently led or carried Evelyn and the rest of the family—Frank, 6; Cedes, 4; Yolanda, 3; Emelio, 2, and 10-months-old Juan—out to the safety of the hallway.

### Nothing Left for Firemen

As a couple of the hoods took the children downstairs, growling reassuringly to them, the rest of the mob ran back into the apartment and went to work as when taking over a joint. With professional finesse, they smashed windows to let the smoke out. They threw a burning mattress down into the street. They broke up the bed

which was also afire and threw the pieces out the window. A burning dresser followed.

When Chief Alexander Steier of the 32d Battalion rolled to the scene with impressive fire-fighting reinforcements, there was nothing left to do except exclaim in amazement.

"They did a good job," Chief Steier said. "When we got there, they had taken care of everything. They had the fire out, and the kids out. A very good job."

Mrs. Biaz came home and showered the hoods with compliments.

"They saved the lives of my children!" she shouted. "They are wonderful boys! God bless them!"

Carried away by their day, the mob went even further.

While Larry, the one who needed medical treatment, was being helped upstairs to his bed at 51 President St., the six other hoods formed a Biaz welfare committee. They arranged for Mrs. Lucy Dellagatta, who owns a luncheonette on the ground floor where the fire occurred and lives in a second-floor apartment there, to take the family temporarily.

### Pool Cash for the Kids

Then they pooled their walking-around money and bought clothes for all the children. After that, they canvassed startled storekeepers along nearby Columbia St. in behalf of an honest cause and raised a sizeable collection.

Assistant Chief Inspector Raymond Martin, in charge of Brooklyn South detectives, who has made a sort of hobby of arresting Galloites as often as possible, was informed of their day's activities.

"Well, I hope the police have made them into decent citizens," he said cautiously. "It just shows that there is some good in everyone."

Kid Blast had the last word.

"With our crummy run of luck," he snorted, "we'll probably be pinched for fighting the fire without a union card."

*Used by permission
New York Daily News,
New York's Picture
Newspaper.*

# SIX

## *Editors and Editing*

WHEN THE EDITOR of *Newsweek* decided to run a cover story on Major General Edwin A. Walker and the "far right wing" in the December 4, 1961, issue, he called upon more than 40 editors, correspondents, researchers, and photographers to put together more than 300,000 words, which were then boiled down to a published article of about 6,000 words. *Newsweek* bureaus in Atlanta, Washington, Chicago, Detroit, San Francisco, and Los Angeles helped to gather facts and interviews, while correspondents in Hong Kong, Berlin, and Tokyo collected more background and caught up with sources who were traveling. Less than two weeks elapsed between the decision to go with the Walker cover story and the publication date. The extensive coverage was necessitated by the editor's belief in objectivity as "a fair, just, dispassionate and equitable grappling with the facts." He estimated the cost of this effort at over $10,000.

## *The Editor: General*

An editor is a person who takes charge of a story from the moment when it first exists as a possible item of news before anyone has gathered or written anything on it. The editor then makes decisions about the story until it reaches the reader or viewer. But *editor* is a broad, general title; under it come many tasks and many responsibilities. The purpose of this chapter is to try to sort out the important ones and establish the special features of each type. Some may appeal to you more than others as ultimate goals of your career in journalism, and some may appeal to you as possible stepping-stones. Let's talk first about editors in general, throughout the media of journalism, and then about some of the editors and editing jobs you will encounter in the different media.

Editorial jobs are *handling* jobs: people-handling and material-handling jobs. The people handling is a matter of assigning people, using a staff so as to take advantage of all its resources and abilities. The material-handling involves working with material that others have developed, whether it be copy on paper or motion-picture film, whether it be a dispatch from the other side of the world or a syndicated column from Washington or a free-lance article for a Sunday feature section. In one sense, the editor is a sort of middleman between the reporter and the public, between the news itself and the public.

An editor is one who supervises the gathering, evaluation, selection, editing, and arrangement of the news—in whatever medium he works. Deciding is his business. He decides whether a story belongs on page one or should lead off a broadcast. He decides whether it merits half a column or half a page, half a minute or half an hour. He decides whether it shall be told with pictures or with text, and with what measure of each. He decides how best to handle the story within his medium. The Gallo brothers story which you read at the end of the previous chapter was reported in other papers but hardly with the same color as the *Daily News.* Even the direct quotes showed that a grammar-minded editor had been over them. An editor decides what typography and makeup will attract and hold the audience which his publication wants and he decides how much time and money to spend in the effort to cover any story properly.

Under pressure of having available far more news and information than he can use, the editor must do his job with a thorough knowledge of the subject, the proper balance between both sides of any story, and the greatest possible completeness. The most important person for him to please, if he is a competent editor with his mind on all his readers, is himself. And in order to please himself and make decisions that are wise in the chaos of the daily grind as well as the long run, he needs to know something about most everything. Faced with different choices as each day's news develops, he must know what to throw out, what to keep, what to treat importantly. For it is his middleman's job to winnow out what is unimportant for the reader or viewer, keep what the reader or viewer will want to know, and relate it to the problems of the day.

Some editors are also men of intelligence and courage, ready and able to take stands and *tell* people what they need to know. Editors have been beaten in the street, and burned in effigy—in the United States, in the 1960's —for taking stands that were unpopular.

Of course, not all editors see the news the same way or agree on what is most important, so what is front page news to one paper may be back page news—or no news— to another. A comparison between two leading papers in our biggest city almost any day will give you some examples, though they won't always be at such opposite poles as on January 24, 1962, when a front page headline in the *New York Times* said:

> ## U.S. IS ADVANCING
> ## PLAN TO SUSPEND
> ## CUBA FROM O.A.S.

and one in the *Herald Tribune* said:

> # U.S. Retreating
> # On Latin Action
> # Against Castro

Or take the coverage of the Kennedy Administration in Washington in 1961. The *Times* editors, sensing important news in the Administration's enthusiasm for the arts, ran a front page story with the four-column head, "*Macbeth* IS PLAYED ON WHITE HOUSE STAGE," a three-column cut of the East Ballroom, a three-column sketch of the room's temporary stage, and a total of close to four full columns telling how Shakespeare came to the White

House (October 5, 1961). The *Herald Tribune,* in half a column on an inside page, reported the state dinner which occasioned the performance but mentioned neither *Macbeth* nor the bard.

Now, what about the editors in the different media? How are they organized to handle their staffs and the volume of material involved in newsgathering?

*Newspaper Editors*

Let's begin with newspapers and consider the typical editorial jobs at a good-sized metropolitan daily. Although no two papers are organized exactly the same way and no two editors have exactly the same working habits, there are general similarities among all papers, large and small, which carry over into the other media. Newspaper methods of handling news and those who gather it are duplicated in many ways in broadcasting, news magazines, and the wire services. Once you have learned the ropes in a newspaper city room, you can make yourself at home pretty easily in any other part of the business.

Suppose you are a reporter on general assignment. Who tells you where to go and what stories to cover? The *city editor,* or one of his deskmen. He directs news coverage for the entire city and suburban area, keeping track of scheduled events and coping quietly and efficiently with hard news when it breaks. He is omniscient in two ways: He knows everything that is going on in town, and he knows everything about the special abilities as well as the weaknesses of his staff. One of his chief tools is the daily assignment sheet, on which he keeps track of each story that is being covered and of the reporter who is on the assignment. Another is his futures book or file, in which he plans assignments and keeps track of coming events.

When hard news is breaking fast, the city editor or the man on the desk may ask you to keep in touch with him by phone. He may have you and several other reporters on the same story, calling in the progress of an astronaut's ticker-tape parade, of a general-alarm fire, or the appearances around town of a political candidate. When you call, he may send you to another position to cover another angle of the story, or ask you to dictate what you've learned to a rewriteman.

When you come back and get your story down on paper, or when your rewriteman cranks it out of his typewriter, it goes first to the city desk, where it is scanned quickly for its relative importance in comparison with other stories. Then it goes to the copy desk.

## The Copy Editor

Of all those who handle the story *after* it has been put on paper, probably the most important is the *copy editor*. Each piece of copy passes under his scrutiny on its way to the composing room to be set into type. His job is to correct errors in fact, grammar, and spelling; make any corrections needed to make the copy conform to the paper's style, catch libelous statements, judge news values in the story, cut the story to the proper length, and write the headline.

While a good set of reference works and a good morgue are important tools of the copy editor, even more essential are a sound education and a vast reservoir of general information. The good copy editor lets nothing get by that is not clear, but he must also have a "feel" for individual style if he is to avoid making changes that stiffen a sentence, violate the author's writing personality, or misinterpret his meaning.

One experienced copy editor has said that each piece of copy must be met on its own terms. It is up to the copy editor to see that it goes on to the reader in the most readable and appropriate guise—saying what the writer meant to say but representing him at his best.

Thus the copy editor gets the story in shape for publication. His final task is to write the *headline*. In a certain number of typographical characters, fitted into a certain number of lines, in upper or lower case, and in a certain typeface and size, the headline sets forth the basic facts of the story, arousing the reader's interest and compelling him to read on into the lead. A good headline captures the spirit of the story by its very look; an italicized upper and lower case two-column head, without additional banks below, promises a relatively light, human-interest story, while a banner headline entirely in upper case across several columns or an entire page, with supplemental banks in a single or double column, signals a major story of great importance.

The headline is the epitome of the paper's style and character. The *Daily News*, as impudent and unawed as its millions of New York readers, knows no public figure too respected or prominent not to be nicknamed in its headlines. *Variety* would be unrecognizable without the language of show biz in its headlines. When the *New York Herald Tribune* underwent a major change in style a while back, critics noted how many of its headlines were written as questions; yet the form was appropriate, for the *Tribune* WAS questioning everything—itself, and the world it reported. The *New York Times* is considered a good gray lady because of its conservative makeup. In every case the style is maintained by good copy editors.

Good copy editing is important to the morale of the entire editorial staff. While a reporter or rewriteman does best to forget his copy once it is written and gone, he cannot help striving to do a better job when he knows his copy is going into the hands of a really competent copy editor. When a managing editor hires a copy editor, only a trial of a week or more will disclose his competence. Generally speaking, of all journalists, copy editors have the best chance of getting work when jobs are scarce.

A good copy editor even knows when to go along with a reporter in breaking all the rules. For example, take the piece on the following page which appeared in the *New York Times* of February 24, 1962.

## BUZZ BUZZ RECITAL GETS A LOUD NO CLAP

Crazy concert was Richard Maxfield yesterday works of Carnegit Recital Hall six happened electronic?

Tapes played, maybe. Sonnywilsonterryjonningsjosephbyrd was jazz go too. Why not. All at once. Buzz, buzz power-saw woodcut; sawdust in a heap. All at once. Reading-paper composer; come, go, people, come, go, talk, go, onstage off, buzz go.

Loud? Too loud? Anyone seen a blue coat says composer?

Round tapes round. Loud speaker loud. Buzz saw buzz. Compose composer poser.

Piano inside, plunk, bang, inside. Why not. Tearing-hair manager, will go piano out of tune; 8:30 my concert next, no, no. Stop piano bang says manager. Why not. Stop.

Good concert, says composer, informal. Clap, clap, clap. No clap. Formal too much says critic. Dinnertime. Good night. Like bad.          **E. S.**

(Copyright *The New York Times.* Used by permission.)

## Other Newspaper Editors

While your city editor is keeping you busy on general assignment, other editors are heading up other areas. In one corner of the newsroom sits the *national editor*, near the banks of teletype machines which clatter out copy from the wire services and from your paper's bureaus in other cities. (At some papers this man is known as the *telegraph editor* or *wire editor*.) He organizes the gathering of news beyond the city, across the country. Where several correspondents staff one bureau, as in Washington, the *bureau chief* is a kind of city editor for that area; he is then responsible to the national editor at headquarters.

The national editor keeps in touch by telephone or teletype, requesting coverage from bureaus or from individual correspondents. Since the latter usually supply stories only on request, or after outlining them and asking how much coverage might be wanted, the national editor needs to keep in touch with a wide variety of events. When a foreign head of state tours the United States or a vast drought sears several states or there is a national election, the national editor's skills in remote control are put to a severe test.

In the daily grind, the stories which come in to the national editor's desk are quickly scanned and turned over to copy editors, the same as local stories.

So are those which come in to the *foreign editor*. This man works by even more remote control, for his stories all come in from beyond the continental United States. And, just as the city editor knows every nook and cranny of the city and every special skill of each general assignment and district man, so the foreign editor keeps abreast of news developments all over the world and sends correspondents best equipped to cover them.

It takes many editors and departments to staff a metropolitan daily. While you are covering general assignments and turning your stories in to the city editor, your colleagues in the *sports* world drop their copy on the sports desk . . . the distaff side of the news is covered by *society* and *women's page* editors and staffs . . . the *arts and amusements* editor reports the world of entertainment . . . and other specialists are directed by the *business and financial,* the *obituary,* or the *industry and labor* editors.

The role of the *picture editor* has become increasingly important. Newspapers use photographs more and more to tell the story, as the magazines do. Fewer and fewer editors rely on the old standbys—the polar bears at the zoo on a hot day, the letters to Santa on the bulletin board backstage at the post office. Some city editors have the final say about which pictures are used, and how. At other papers, the picture editor has full responsibility; more than a mere cutline writer and picture sizer who knows the mechanics of his business, he is in effect a director of graphic arts.

The picture editor, like other editors, has not only a news-handling but a people-handling job. He understands that getting a good picture is often as difficult as getting a good story: It requires legwork, digging and checking out sources, a knowledge of news values as well as photography, and a sense of timing even more sensitive than a reporter's. Getting the good pictures takes time. While you can still find city editors who think one afternoon will do to get photographs for a feature on which a reporter has spent three weeks, such an unenlightened viewpoint is becoming rare. One paper, the *Charlotte News and*

*Observer*, sends photographers out on "open assignment," telling them to take as much time as they need to bring in whatever picture stories they happen to see around the city. About one third of the pictures used in the paper come from such assignments.

As each story leaves its copy editor and moves on to the composing room, one duplicate is sent back to the appropriate editor. With a complete file of the stories his department is preparing, he is able to judge which deserve consideration for the front page, which must even now be spiked on the dead hook, and which are likely to wind up in the overset. He goes to the daily news conference with a complete picture of the news up to this moment in his field.

Remember our visit to the news conference, in Chapter One? The man in charge is the boss of all the editors we have been discussing: the *managing editor*. He is not only in charge of the news conference; he is in charge of the news, and of the newspaper. For the managing editor, more than any other single person, manages the news and the people who gather it and is responsible to the owner or publisher.

Applying his news sense, the managing editor weighs the bids of all the other editors for front page space or greater space on inside pages. He decides on the extent of special coverage for major stories. His direction sets the tone and style of the paper. At the same time, he is responsible for maintaining a competent staff to turn out the paper; he hires and fires, and manages raises in pay and promotions. In the world beyond his paper, he often is the busiest speechmaker and luncheon attender of the entire staff. To the business and professional community, he may be the best known representative of his paper, while to the man on the street he is an unknown, though many of his reporters are familiar names to his readers. Unlike any of his editors, he is besieged by people who have something to sell—a new feature or cartoon or syndicated column.

At many papers, the managing editor or one of his assistants is responsible for daily decisions about the play of stories on the front page. At others, the *news editor* is the major decision maker in the makeup of the paper and is a kind of chief copy editor, responsible for style and content but not for operations.

If it is a morning paper, often a *night editor* takes charge after the news conference has been held, and guides the editing and printing which occur through the evening while the world is quieting down and after the reporters and early rewritemen who have completed their shifts have left for the day. Probably the city editor and managing editor have departed, too, leaving the night editor to put the paper to bed and cope with any news that breaks late. Thus, on late stories the night editor must combine the abilities of each of the department heads and city, national, and foreign editors.

How do editorials get written? At smaller newspapers, the editor himself usually writes them when he has time and when he feels compelled to speak out on some issue. The result is an editorial style distinctively his own. At larger newspapers, there is usually an editorial board or staff of editorial writers, most of whom are specialists in city, state, or national affairs, or in such subjects as politics and labor. Daily editorial conferences of these writers are held. At some papers, policy on specific issues is discussed and set, sometimes by vote. When editorial subject matter has been agreed upon, the writer best equipped for the subject then produces the editorial. At other papers, this system is considered too restrictive; here, the editor simply finds out what topics each member of the editorial board wants to write about, reserving the vote on policy only for major issues.

The character of a paper, or its point of view—Republican or Democratic or Independent, liberal or conservative —is set by its editorial position over a period of time. Where the paper is dominated by an individualistic publisher, that publisher's views will obviously set the tone and policy of the editorials. But most editorial boards are independent of direct rule by their publishers, and their daily editorials represent their best judgment, within the framework of the paper's established character, on current topics.

These, then, are the journalists who pick out what's important, digest it, and without partisanship or prejudice relate it to the problems of the day. Their desks and duties are roughly paralleled in the worlds of broadcasting, news magazines, and wire services.

## *Editors in Broadcasting*

Perhaps because it is a younger medium and not as settled in its ways, broadcast news has not developed titles that apply throughout the business. Editors who do the same work may not have the same titles at NBC as at CBS or at a local station. However, the *news director* is almost always the man, like the newspaper's managing editor, who is responsible for deciding what to cover and how to cover it, whether in a regular newscast, a quick bulletin, or a special documentary. The same person may also be known as *director of news and special events* or *news supervisor*. Sometimes a special program, such as NBC's *Today,* has an editor who is called *associate producer of news.* This involves a function unique to an editor in broadcasting: Like the producer of any play or motion picture or TV show, he creates a climate in which an assortment of skilled and talented people can work together. He is master of logistics, moving highly paid crews with bulky equipment to the right place at the right time, and he weighs the importance of the news against the complications of the logistics. Then there's the network *TV assignments editor.* Like the national editor on a paper, he decides how coverage of national stories around the country will be handled for the network newscasts; he may order a crew from New York to the scene, and sometimes he asks for coverage by the nearest station affiliated with the network. At NBC the *editor of news* is somewhat comparable to an editor of a newspaper. He worries about substance—content, style, pronunciation, *what* is going on the air—rather than operations or *how* the coverage is obtained.

Radio and TV stations go all out when hard news breaks. An *Andrea Doria* sinking off Nantucket, a midair collision of two giant passenger planes over New York, a vast forest fire sweeping over the ridges and canyons near the homes of Los Angeles residents—these bring to the airwaves the fullest kind of coverage, with interviews, airviews, background footage, and live coverage all edited together.

Other hard news has been ignored. "Television from time to time has been quite occupied with crime and yet there has been no genuine crime reporting on TV," says Fred W. Friendly, executive producer of *CBS Reports*. "Newspapers have been doing it for generations and I'd like to see us cover 'city-side' news, too." (The *New York Times*, November 24, 1961.) For a start, Friendly broadcast "Biography of a Bookie Joint," so candid an examination of a gambling house that other members of the press charged that the network had been tipped off in advance of a raid.

## Magazine Editors

Editors of a news magazine have special problems of their own. Magazines can do some things that newspapers and other media cannot. Since they are published weekly or monthly, they can often wrap up an entire story, from beginning to end, in one issue. They can provide greater breadth and depth, more interpretation, because they view the story as a whole rather than in daily or hourly segments. And, because they are edited for an audience that is national in scope and homogeneous in thought, rather than geographically local and heterogeneous in thought, they have the opportunity to exhibit a special kind of leadership.

News magazines have a way of departmentalizing the news. Their editors are department heads, directing staffs of specialists.

Because the news magazine editor is not under daily deadline pressure, he has time to use the conference as a working tool. Rounding up the many stories from domestic and foreign correspondents, the wire services, and from other publications, he sits down in a story conference with departmental editors to pick the top stories that are to be researched further and then written. Often the direction of the writing comes out of the story conference, and sometimes a policy line on a major story is handed down from the magazine's top management.

With no bylines and few datelines to authenticate the source, it is the editor's task to convey the impression that the magazine is speaking from its headquarters, rather than a reporter filing a story from the scene. Thus, *U. S. News & World Report* writes its interview articles in question and answer style but reveals only who is giving the answers, not who is asking the questions. With the finished story being written at headquarters and with a week between deadlines, the magazine editor has been known to encourage competition between departments; for a feature story about a Hollywood movie queen's home life, for instance, he might assign both the show business writers and the modern living writers, to see which group would come up with the most interesting approach to the subject.

### The Community Editor

Of all the editors we have glimpsed, which would you rather be? Or would you rather be all of then—rolled into one? If so, you're headed for a weekly or community newspaper. This does not necessarily mean that you must plan to live in a small town far out in the country. As we noted in Chapter Two, plenty of community weeklies are found in the thickly populated metropolitan areas, and on their suburban fringes.

Neither the big city dailies nor TV and radio provide the kind of local coverage that comes weekly in this paper— the story of every auto accident, every wedding, every death, every PTA or Board of Estimate meeting. Such news is sought whether the reader's neighborhood is Greenwich Village or Morningside Heights in Manhattan or a town of five thousand in Iowa. As the editor supplying your neighbors with the news of their neighbors, and of their schools and clubs and churches and government, you are a sort of applied social scientist working with the community's many forces and interests, giving the reader an identity he needs. Your paper provides a medium of debate on local issues, reporting and interpreting all sides, and taking its own stand in editorial comment, as well as opening its columns to letters and local columnists.

At a community weekly, the entire editorial staff often consists of only one or two reporters, a woman to head up the personal, social, and women's news, and a handful of part-time stringers. So you are all kinds of editor rolled into one—copy editor, city editor, managing editor, editorial writer. Since you are probably part owner of the paper, you had better also be a good businessman.

To be in charge of all the news, and of all the people who

handle it, in any size operation in any medium is a feverish task. Carl Lindstrom, former editor of the *Hartford Times*, has set the tone of the editor's high calling:

Our parlous times cry out for the responsible editor. I don't mean the editorial job holder, the man with a title on his office door, but the man who has the ability to think and the courage to face his conclusions. In this day when mainly those things that can maintain themselves by propaganda are in the ascendancy I know of no remedy for purifying the stream of news except editorial integrity. This is the hour for the bold man, the free man. His name is editor!

(Carl E. Lindstrom, "The Technique of Journalism," Buckland Memorial Lecture, Ryerson Institute of Technology, Toronto, February 20, 1962.)

# SEVEN

## Specialists and Others

THIS IS AN AGE of specialists in journalism as elsewhere. While it is a fine thing to be able to cover any story well, there is simply too much going on in the world today for every reporter to be able to become an instant authority as soon as he gets an assignment, or for him to be able to write it in terms that make the subject clear to his reader without talking down to him. If you have the wide range of interests that makes you want to be a newsman in the first place, you are likely to have one or two special interests. Cultivate them. When your job is to inform, there is little more rewarding than the effort to know your subject well.

### The Specialists

There are many specialties in journalism. The field of *government and politics* requires insight into the workings of city halls and state capitols; and the Washington press corps makes unique demands on its members, not only for skill, knowledge, and experience—the ability to ask the penetrating question, but also the discretion to know how to use the answer.

*Court reporting*, from traffic court to the highest in the land, calls for other skills, though the United States Supreme Court, one of our three branches of government, has been pretty well neglected by editors as an area of specialization.

Still waiting for an adequate number of newsmen adequately equipped to report all its doings is the *United Nations*; at present, only the New York newspapers and the wire services staff the UN press corps with the kind of specialists many feel it deserves. *Industry and labor, welfare* and *education*, call for specialized knowledge. *Religion* is a beat, too; more than just reporting a batch of sermons each Monday morning, it competes daily for space and position with other stories. Then there are the *arts* and *entertainment*. In 1962, the *New York Times* established the position of *cultural news director*, an editorship in charge of art, music, dance, drama, radio and television, motion pictures, and books. *Fashion* is a world of its own—and is there any wider world than *home and food news*? *Obituaries*? You can compile them like grocery lists, or you can specialize in making them readable tributes to the deceased. If you specialize in business news, chances are you will find your niche in business publications, for only the wire services and a handful of major dailies offer a real business-financial section to the general reader.

*Science* is the most prominent speciality today, but, while good science reporters are now developing, it is by no means certain that enough specialization in science has occurred among editors. Some other specialties depend on where you are. In New York, the *transport news editor* of the *Times* has a staff of ten men just to cover the waterborne shipping, aviation, and trucking industries. You won't find quite such a job in Arizona—but there a special knowledge of irrigation and its industrial and farming applications might come in handy.

Specialization may involve elements other than writing and editing. Great news pictures live in a way that great news dispatches never do, whether of an East German soldier leaping rolls of barbed wire to freedom or of Mrs. Kennedy pitching headlong over a fence. The photojournalist needs the presence of mind to know when the news picture may occur (as did the photographers at the Berlin wall and on the Virginia fox-hunting grounds), the technical ability to get the picture that can never be repeated, and the reportorial ability to get it in a way that tells the story. Thus the key word for news photographers is *readiness.*

They must use good judgment just as much as reporters and usually they must be quicker on their feet. Says the picture caption: "Seeing newsmen gathered outside his physician's office and not wishing to draw attention to his presence, the duke [of Windsor] quietly left via a fire escape out back. But one news photographer outsmarted him and took his picture." The duke's visit to his doctor for a routine checkup had little news value and no pictorial value on the face of it, but it made an entertaining full-page shot in a picture magazine when the duke tried to evade the press.

Sometimes the news photographer gets a memorable

picture not only because he is at the right place at the
right time but because he notices details that the average
person or average news photographer might overlook.
Such was the case with the picture of Jacqueline Kennedy
pitching headlong off a horse. Besides being a good photojournalist, the photographer was an excellent horseman.
He attended the hunt on a Virginia estate because Mrs.
Kennedy was riding and his news sense told him a good
picture story might develop.

Stationing himself at a difficult jump, he noticed as the
First Lady approached that her horse was twisting its tail
in a way that jumping horses do when they don't like
what's coming next. The photographer raised his camera,
waited patiently a few seconds, and caught the picture of
Mrs. Kennedy as she sailed over the fence when the horse
balked. Passing up the chance to take more pictures of
Mrs. Kennedy on the ground, he hurried to her assistance.
Later he released the picture for publication after receiving Mrs. Kennedy's personal approval, and with the
stipulation that it would appear only with a second photograph showing her remounted and unhurt.

Another group of journalists inform and interpret
without words or photographs. They are the *artists* who
draw maps and diagrams to illustrate news stories, and the
*cartoonists* who use humor to comment on current situations. While at many newspapers the cartoonist illustrates
the day's major editorial, at others he is given free rein
to turn to any subject he wishes.

An important arm of the editorial department, serving

reporters, rewritemen, and editors is the *library*. Ideally, its files contain reference books and clippings on every subject imaginable, dating back to the day the publication first opened an office and set aside a corner for research. The *New York Times* library employs more than 80 persons, contains more than 35,000 books, and countless clips. Nearly an entire floor of the new Time & Life Building in New York is devoted to the library, with about 75 per cent of the space taken up by file cabinets indexed by subject. This is work for trained librarians who are journalists in mind and heart, for the library is useless if it is not able to supply complete information quickly.

## *Women in Journalism*

Journalism has been a man's world for a long time. Working newsmen outnumber working newswomen and many have a decided prejudice against them. To break into this man's world is a real challenge. Unfortunately, many young women who do manage to break into the field often seem to do so at the expense of the very charm that might help them most in the business. "They let their femininity go," is the way one newswoman puts it.

An indication of how men look on the problem may be seen in the fact that the National Press Club in Washington, an all-male organization, seats visiting women reporters in the balcony when foreign dignitaries speak or give press conferences at the club.

The Columbia School of Journalism accepts only a limited number of women because of the difficulty they will have in finding jobs. Across the country, Stanford Uni-

versity frankly states that the proportion of positions on
newspapers open to women is limited and that the number
of magazines on the Pacific Coast is limited. The journalism department takes these facts into consideration in
the acceptance of women majors in the subject. Bernard
Kilgore, publisher of the *Wall Street Journal*, has said,
"Our managing editor has a prejudice against women.
Women don't make a career of it. They don't stay too
long, and we are desperately anxious to develop subexecu-
tives. Women should try to work for the smaller newspaper." (*Editor & Publisher*, February 17, 1962, p. 11.)

Of two hundred wire service journalists in New York,
maybe half a dozen are women. Of about seventy journalists in NBC's New York news department, two are
women. The *New York Times* has copy boys but, at last
count, only one copy girl. Yet women do go into journalism
and thrive; in Warren, Pennsylvania, Joy Owens is sports
editor of the *Times-Mirror*. Where the audience is women,
though, women are expected to be in charge. It is hardly
surprising that they generally handle fashions and food
and society news. However, young women will find more
opportunities in public relations.

*Public Relations and Press Agents*

Of three basic areas of public relations in which the
qualified journalist may seek his goals, one is known as
*corporate public relations*—although it does not speak
only for corporations. The other areas may be described as
*industrial journalism* and *government public relations*.

It is not many years since most journalists looked down

on the press agent, and a good number still do. But newspapers, magazines, and radio and TV could barely function today without public relations people. They depend on a steady stream of press releases. In fact, today's editor may need the press agent more than the press agent needs the editor.

Press releases arrive at the bigger media and wire services by the bushel. (One study showed that one New York newspaper receives 8,300 press releases weekly.) Well over half the stories and features that get on the air and into the papers are supplied by public relations sources. No wonder, then, that businessmen, in the attempt to get their stories to the public, turn to qualified journalists to handle their public relations. Some maintain their own PR staffs, some commission public relations firms, and some do both.

Good newsmen make good PR men if they retain their independence of thought, their curiosity, and their skepticism. But in this end of the business you are paid to let the public know the good things your client is doing and, usually, to keep the bad things unknown. Knowing when and how *not* to submit your client to the public view is a vital public relations skill, and in the process you may have to close an eye to your objective viewpoint. Some who hire press agents do so because they feel they can't handle the press without professional help. Finding themselves in the spotlight for one reason or another, they are awestruck and concerned about how they will be treated.

The newspaperman's ability to find a good angle for a story is the press agent's main asset. If you were the press

agent for the New York City Housing Authority, how
would you get as ordinary an event as a ground-breaking
onto the front pages against the competition of Soviet
nuclear weapons tests, a citywide election, a storm over a
Peace Corps girl's postcard, and (a publicity stunt already
riding high) the visit of Lyndon Johnson's camel driver
from Pakistan?

Oscar Kanny put on his thinking cap when it came time
for the dedication of an East Harlem housing project
named for the late Senator Robert A. Taft. Senator Taft
had gone to Yale—and so had four of those who joined
in the dedication: Mayor Wagner, Park Commissioner
Newbold Morris, Senator Prescott Bush of Connecticut,
and Robert Moses. At the dedication, Kanny arranged for
them to join a group of Yale alumni Whiffenpoofs in
singing "Mother of Man" and "The Whiffenpoof Song."
"Who ever heard or saw Bob Moses sing?" asked Kanny,
as his story cornered three front page columns of the
*New York Times,* four spots in TV newscasts, distribution
to eighteen papers by the *Chicago Tribune* feature service,
and the front page of the *New York Daily News.* Said
Kanny, "This is what everybody dreams of!"


WANTED: Editor. Must have helicopter pilot's license.


So read a classified advertisement. A printer's error?
No. A company manufacturing helicopters wanted an
editor for its house organ. The man who got the job went
into *industrial journalism.*

Actually, industrial journalists don't like the term

"house organ." They prefer "employee publication." But that is only one of the areas in which you operate in this field. From getting out the weekly or monthly paper or magazine for employees, you may turn to community relationships. This means putting out information about your firm or client's relationship with the community in which it is located, including everything from smoke abatement to the company softball team. If your assignment is press services, you develop stories and send releases to both the trade and general press. Or, the company's annual report or publicity for the company's products may be your worry. To give you an idea of what fine lines may be drawn: At General Foods in White Plains, home office of a major corporation manufacturing many different food items, female industrial journalists are assigned to the kitchens as a special staff, to work primarily with food editors (getting out recipes and information on new products), while male industrial journalists work strictly with the grocery trade and its publications.

## Government Public Relations

Getting to Washington is the ambition of many a young man and woman in journalism, and, in a country where freedom of the press is guaranteed by the Constitution, there can be no more rewarding task than reporting the workings of democracy. But with an interest in Washington must come an understanding of the practice of government public relations.

Not everybody approves of it. One editor has remarked, "The concentration of press agents and public relations

counselors in the United States Government, state governments, and local governments is, in my judgment, inde-
fensible and disgraceful." (Louis Seltzer of the *Cleveland
Press* on "Death in the City Room," CBS Television,
January 25, 1962.) In Washington, this concentration
amounts to nearly three thousand government information
officers—more than double the size of the Washington press
corps. Every Congressman, department, and bureau has
its information officer or staff. Senators and bureau
chiefs get out mimeographed press releases daily, stating
their positions on issues. The press release is only one
device. There is also the press conference, the official
"leak," the not-for-attribution briefing, and the trial
balloon.

Why all this? Because the government official's problem
is not only to make policy and develop programs but to put
them over. He must stimulate political support for his
actions, and publicity is one of his best ways of getting that
support. So, like the corporation, the government official
looks to experts in the techniques of journalism to put
across his point of view.

The working press is there, ready and waiting. In each
house of Congress, the press gallery hangs over the
chamber, directly connected with the outside world through
muted telephones, while teletype machines wait just across
the hall. At the White House, the pressroom is right beside the entrance to the executive wing, and nearly thirty
reporters whose sole assignment is this beat attend their
typewriters, telephones, and poker tables. In committee
meetings, photographers squat at the table edge, within

arm's reach of the witnesses, while the bright lights needed for television filming illuminate the scene. The ultimate advantage of this power of publicity was taken by the late Senator Joseph R. McCarthy, a master at abusing the relationship. Let Richard H. Rovere, a reporter who was there during the McCarthy era, describe it for you:

For publicity, McCarthy had a talent unmatched by any other politician of this century. He knew the newspapermen and how and when they worked and what they needed and when their deadlines were, and what made a "lead," what made an "overnight," what made a "sidebar." He knew how to "top" or "blanket" a story unfavorable to him. McCarthy always knew what he was up to. He knew, on his good days, how to make a story out of nothing and he knew how to back into somebody else's story. . . . When Nathan Pusey became President of Harvard University, he was all ready with a comment: "I do not think Dr. Pusey is or has been a member of the Communist Party." . . . He knew how to get into the news even on those rare occasions when invention failed him and he had no "unfacts" to give out. For example, he invented the morning press conference called for the purpose of announcing an afternoon press conference. . . . To reporters. . . McCarthy said, "You looking for a story?"

"Sure, you got one?"

McCarthy: "Mmmm, now, let's see. . . . I'll give you something. You can say that I'm going to subpoena Harry Truman."

Of course, it never happened—that is to say, Truman never testified, but the story got into print, even though the reporters to whom it was given were angry about the system that required them to publish "news" they knew to be fraudulent, but prohibited them from reporting their knowledge of its fraudulence. (Richard H. Rovere, *Senator Joe McCarthy*, New York: Harcourt, Brace & Co., 1959.)

The problem of journalism versus government public relations, which ideally ought not to be a "versus" problem, has been well summed up by Laurence Barrett, who covers City Hall for the *New York Herald Tribune*:

It appears that the third Wagner administration regards reporters much as health officials regarded Typhoid Mary. . . . The expanded, higher-priced public relations team brought in two months ago now is functioning smoothly. Publicity releases rain on the pressroom like confetti at an astronaut's parade. They are not a substitute for news, however.

In the old days, reporters could nearly always see the Mayor when they wanted to—that is, when breaking news required the publication of the city's position, as set forth by its highest official. . . .

Press conferences now are fewer in number. Frequently the Mayor will not see reporters when an issue is hot. . . .

Reliance on the prepared statement is another innovation. . . This discourages questioning. . . .

On Friday, for instance, Mr. Wagner . . . read a prepared statement of considerable complexity, gave newspaper reporters about five minutes for questions, took his statement to the cameras and microphones and declined to answer any questions at all for radio and television.

This type of operation cannot be called a press conference in the accepted sense of the term. It might make for less work by reporters. It also gives the public less information. (The *New York Herald Tribune*, March 5, 1962.)

For a close look at the operation of government public relations at the very top, take the Presidential press conference. It is now customary to broadcast these conferences live on TV and radio; they are extensively reported in the bigger newspapers, and the *New York Times,* for one, prints the verbatim transcript.

"The real use of the Presidential press conference," said Walter Lippmann in his syndicated column on March 7, 1961, "is to enable the President to explain his policies and, if necessary, to compel him to explain them. In any event, explanation, not announcements or scoops, is wanted in this extremely public but also very intimate encounter between the President and the public."

The Presidential press conference is not only an intimate encounter between the President and the press, it is also one for which the President tries to be thoroughly prepared. Briefed by his press secretary and members of his Cabinet beforehand, he goes over more than eighty questions that might be asked—three times as many as could be asked in the usual thirty-minute conference.

President Kennedy's relationship with the press is also unique because he is probably more interested in journalism and more conscious of the power of the press than any President in history. Once a journalist himself, he met his wife, a press photographer at the time, in the home of a Washington correspondent. He dines at reporters' houses, invites editors to lunch, and makes the White House more accessible to reporters than ever before.

"He is his own best public relations man," says Presidential press secretary Pierre Salinger.

If you want to go into journalism, you might keep an eye on the President. You can learn a lot from him, and from his press secretary, too.

## The Foreign Correspondent

Like getting to Washington, getting overseas and into the role of *foreign correspondent* is often the goal of the young journalist. Young reporters in responsible foreign berths are hard to find. Veteran newsmen are almost always preferred.

The foreign correspondent files many more stories than are used. Back home, his foreign editor sifts through them and decides, from his viewpoint on the American mainland, what is important enough to run. His decision is affected by the importance of news from other foreign correspondents and by the amount and importance of domestic news.

For differing reasons, the foreign correspondent doesn't always make his editor aware of what is significant. In late 1961 and early 1962, when every attempt to breach or leap the Berlin wall was receiving dramatic play in the United States press, European papers were full of the story of how a sleeping pill had caused deformities in several thousand European babies. The story received little notice in America until July 1962 when a Washington reporter saw the drama of an American doctor's fight to keep the drug off the market until it had been adequately tested.

Either foreign correspondents or their editors back home failed to see, in an age of swift and easy travel throughout the world, the significance of telling Americans about the pill's tragic effect in Europe.

## Columnist, Critic, and Free-Lance

There are journalists whom we might call rugged individualists. And they are of two kinds: *free-lance writers* and *columnists*.

Since three-quarters of what magazines publish today is nonfiction, they depend for much of their material on free-lance writers.

Sometimes the free-lancer is employed in a regular job, and does his free-lance writing in his spare time. In many cases, you will find him in a rather specialized public relations job, such as product publicity. Not so often do you find a journalist in a full-time news getting job who also does much free-lance work on the side. With nearly two hundred members, the Society of Magazine Writers is the organization of the country's major free-lance nonfiction writers.

The daily *columnist* usually works for a syndicate and he works under the dual pressure of self-starting and the deadline. He must grind out several hundred words every day, and he has no editor to give him assignments.

The columnist is a kind of throwback to the era of personal journalism. He writes to please himself and, if he writes intelligently, with a lively touch, he has a following of readers. When he becomes a Walter Lippmann or a Joseph Alsop, he may discover that he has more impact on his readers than do the editorials which flank his column.

One specialist who often has a very direct effect upon his audience—and upon the fortunes of other people—is the *critic*. People buy books or don't, see plays and movies or don't, and decide where to eat or not because of what the critics say.

The most noted fields of criticism in the news media are the theater, motion picture, television and radio, and books. But the opera, the dance, art and music are important fields, too. Whatever the field, the critic's job is first of all a reporting job and the best critics have been reporters at one time or another. The critic has straight facts to report: what happened, who was involved, why and how it happened, the same as in any news story. A high level of knowledgeability is needed, because the critic is often reporting to an audience which knows the subject as well as he does and because the critic is reporting his own reaction, based upon his experience and his knowledge of the field. This is a highly personal kind of reporting and the critic is careful not to be influenced by the opinions of others, including other critics.

# EIGHT

## *Publishers and Others*

"PUBLISHERS ARE a peculiar breed," says CBS newsman Ned Calmer. "They are owners—which distinguishes them from the working stiff in journalism— and from most of their readers—by the widest of gaps." ("WCBS-TV Views the Press," April 29, 1962.)

Publishers are businessmen working for a profit and the publisher's office is seldom the ultimate goal of the working reporter. The publisher's work is executive work, while journalism's basic attraction is writing and reporting and editing.

Sometimes, however, the man at the publisher's desk is someone who has come up through success in editing, and has taken advantage of a chance to buy into the ownership. Such is still the case with many weekly papers that are small enough for a man to own and edit and be his own boss. Often the publisher has come along from success in other businesses and bought out the ownership—frequently to add to his chain.

Whether he is the publisher of a newspaper or the manager of a radio or TV station (and for the sake of this discussion let's include broadcasting executives as "publishers"), it is this man's task to make advertising and circulation sales produce enough revenue to more than offset the expense of producing the paper or magazine or broadcast and thus return a profit to the owner. (The owner may be one person, a group of employees, a closed corporation, or the public, through the sale of stock. One important business, the Associated Press, is a cooperative enterprise jointly owned by its member media and is theoretically a nonprofit organization.)

Usually a *business manager* is responsible for business and mechanical departments, a *controller* for accounting operations (with *auditor, cashier, purchasing agent, credit manager* directing how and where the money comes and goes), a *personnel director* for employee relations, and a *production manager* for getting the product out. The work of each is similar to that in any business organization.

The *advertising director*, with his assistants for *national, local,* and *classified* advertising—or for *network, regional, local, film, tape,* or *live,* at a station or network—is responsible for selling advertising space or time by proving the effectiveness of his publication in reaching the people to whom the advertiser hopes to sell his product or service. The *circulation manager* is responsible for reaching those people, through subscriptions or newsstand sales. (Since the broadcasting audience does not subscribe, this job is confined to the printed media.) He is also responsible for getting the product to the customer: Prompt delivery to the newsstand or to the subscriber's mailbox is his worry.

Within the business department of newspapers, magazines, and broadcasting stations are others who are "in journalism" by dint of their connection with these media, but whose specialties might be applied to other businesses equally well.

It is the job of the *promotion department* to increase circulation, to draw the attention of the viewing or listening public to various features of the publication, to develop sales incentives for salesmen and dealers by creating special offers or contests. It may also dream up various devices to support advertising run by the station or publication.

Public service or institutional promotion also underlines the civic-minded aspects of publications—from the *New York Herald Tribune* Fresh Air Fund to the *Times* Hundred Neediest Cases, and the many soap box derbies sponsored by newspapers.

Major publications and broadcasters employ staff *attorneys* to cope with daily legal problems. Major newspapers own vast tracts of forest and large paper mills, usually hundreds if not thousands of miles from the press room, from which tons of newsprint must arrive daily. Managing this traffic is a vital if thankless job. Major magazines are printed simultaneously at several plants around the United States; to put *Time* on every newsstand and in every subscriber's mailbox on the same day is to accomplish a logistics miracle weekly.

The publisher's obligation to his balance sheet causes him to publish that which gets circulation, to broadcast that which attracts his audience. Yet his obligation to the public demands fearless journalism—news and information which is several cuts above that which merely gets circulation. If your career should eventually take you to the publisher's desk, the reality of this paradox will hit you every day. When it does, whether you turn for help to the "working stiffs" in journalism or to the inventors of contests and dollar-bill-serial-number lotteries may depend on whether you follow the words of a man who has been through it all before: "The best—and cheapest—box office attraction for a newspaper is good news and editorial content." (Mark Ethridge, "The Press," interview on *The American Character*, Center for the Study of Democratic Institutions, The Fund for the Republic, Inc., December, 1961.)

# NINE

# ⭐ *Advice and Devices*

JOURNALISTS ARE always ready to give advice to the neophyte, and to cite experiences others have had in launching their careers. Not everyone agrees about the best places to start—and the best places are not always the easiest places to get into. Many things influence your choice of a starting place and your decisions about what to do during your early years—including whether or not you attended journalism school, your financial situation, the problem of military service, your marital status, and the extracurricular or summer job experience you bring to journalism.

## First Jobs

The jobs are there. In a recent survey of fifty-eight of the largest journalism schools, all but six reported more jobs available than there were graduates to fill them, with the ratio anywhere from three to ten jobs per graduate, and four of the remaining six reported as many jobs available as graduates. While the majority of these jobs were in the bona fide media of journalism, a number of them probably were in the related field of advertising. On the other hand, a graduate of Missouri has been known to have his choice of as many as four newspaper jobs in three states.

A survey of Columbia journalism graduates who have been out from two to eleven years reveals a distinct pattern. While 70 per cent first went into newspapers and wire services, only 48 per cent are still with those media. But the number in magazines, public relations, and radio and TV has increased; the percentage in magazines has doubled, and that in PR has more than doubled. So the trend is into newspapers for the first job, then out of newspapers into other media. It is likely that an even higher percentage of non-journalism-school graduates find the newspaper the best training ground for other media; at the same time, a good many journalism graduates now leap-frog directly into PR, broadcasting, and magazines.

If you start at a weekly paper, you will get a chance to do all the jobs, reporting on a variety of subjects, taking pictures, editing copy, even at times setting type and helping with circulation. In community journalism, openings keep occurring as young people gain experience and move on to higher pay and greater responsibility.

But some older journalists will advise you to start low on the totem pole at an urban daily. This usually means starting off as a copy boy. Here you will be an apprentice in the Old World sense: a flunky who keeps the pastepots filled and copy paper moving between the reporters' or rewritemen's typewriters and the copy desk and the editors and the composing room. If you are a copy boy who is soon to become a reporter, you should keep your eyes and ears open.

When you become a clerk or *cub reporter,* you will be doing clerical work on the news desk, assisting an editor or reporter, sorting out copy, correcting garbled matter in wire stories. You begin to produce for the paper— summarizing speeches, adding further details to obituaries on file for future use, lining up the TV schedules and the stock market tables for the back pages. And at last you go out on a beat with an experienced reporter and then on your own assignments.

College graduates at Time Inc. start in the mail room, then move into research. Movement upward from copy boy is slow at the big metropolitan daily; with a master's degree from Columbia in your hip pocket, you can go into the *New York Times* as a copy boy, and emerge four or five years later as a full-fledged reporter.

Between community journalism's chance to do everything and the big metropolitan daily's chance to run copy lies a dangerous land: the small or medium-sized daily paper. If it is the kind of paper that depends largely on the wire services for most of its news, it will give you the opportunity mainly to handle routine chores—and to continue handling them, in a rut that you should avoid. So study the paper you hope to go to work for. Analyze its local news coverage, its local interpretation of nonlocal news, its employment of specialists, whether it maintains a Washington bureau and any overseas correspondents.

You *can* start in a training program which includes more formal *instruction* than the copy boy program offers.

When you are a copy boy, you learn what you happen to be exposed to or are enterprising enough to dig into, and you move up when you seem to be worth moving up. When you are a trainee in such a program as that maintained by the Gannett News Service, in Rochester, New York, you pursue a formal thirteen-week training course, with assigned lessons and reports.

What about starting with a wire service? If you can demonstrate ability and have some previous experience—with student publications, part-time work, or as a journalism student—a job in a wire service line bureau is one of the finest kinds of apprenticeship. For one thing, you learn to write *fast*. For another, you get used to the idea that journalism can involve a busy eight-hour day, like any other job. Wire service hiring is done by bureau heads around the country.

### Journalism in Uniform

Since you may have to spend some time in the military service, it is possible the service will offer you your first job in journalism. *Public information officers* as well as enlisted men with "journalist" ratings serve in each branch of the armed forces. They get these billets by chance as well as by assignment.

One young ensign serving his two-year tour after graduation from college, where he had majored in journalism, volunteered to do collateral duty as PIO aboard his cruiser. His good work on this extra duty shortly earned him an appointment as full-time PIO. Among his duties was the editing of the ship's paper—a cruiser carries regular wire service teletypes and its daily paper provides the only source of the world's news during long periods at sea.

In domestic ports of call, it was his job to get sailors' names into the news. When he discovered men named Ache, Hurt, and Payne aboard ship, he posed them for a photo in sick bay and happily saw it picked up by AP Wirephoto and Black Star Photo Service. When one thousand midshipmen came aboard for a training cruise, it was his job to send a photo and press release to each midshipman's hometown newspaper. His staff of enlisted men included three who had journalist ratings and three who had photographer ratings.

Currently, the Navy lists about 550 enlisted journalists and 80 officer specialists. Requirements for formal assignment to this special duty are degrees in journalism or media relations, plus three years as a line officer, so the opportunity seems limited. Yet the example we have just cited shows that a young officer can make a place for himself as a PIO.

The Coast Guard has 20 journalism assignments. In the Marines, information services officers are assigned to duty as an additional occupation to that in which they are trained; a journalism career in the regular commissioned rank is rare. But enlisted recruits who have had journalism experience or show potential for informational work are assigned basic military occupational specialties in the informational services field. In addition, the Marine Corps takes about 40 graduates a year from the Navy's School of Journalism at Great Lakes, Illinois.

In training journalists, the Navy school ventures largely into the theory of communications. But applied, practical training is given to men from *all* branches of the service at the U. S. Army Information School at Fort Slocum, New York. Of 150 to 200 men in each of four enlisted classes each year, about 60 per cent are in the Reserve Force Army, serving either for two years or six months of active duty. If, at the time of enlistment or induction, you request assignment to the information field, the Army makes an *enlistment commitment* and is obliged to send you (after eight weeks of basic training) to Fort Slocum. Even if you do not pass the entrance examinations (in spelling, typing, grammar, and American history, plus the clerical test which is one of a number of aptitude tests administered to all soldiers at the beginning of basic training), the Army Information School is obliged to accept you and make every effort to help you pass the courses—*if* you have the enlistment commitment.

Though run by the Army, Fort Slocum is the school to which you go for advanced training for information services assignment—whatever your branch of the armed forces. Besides the four enlisted classes yearly, there are five officer classes, in subjects covering two broad areas. Internal information is directed to those in the service, in the belief that the best source of information is a well-informed soldier. External information is like public relations: It applies to the public whatever policy on information the Defense Department develops and sets forth.

Since military policy on public information varies with

each branch of the service, and may vary widely depending on special circumstances, the subject is taught in detail. When the local police chief roars into the base to demand custody of a serviceman, and charges all manner of crimes against him, or when the local newspaper calls to say it hears the base is storing poison gas, the headache falls not only to the commandant but to the public information officer. He needs to be trained to cope with every eventuality, in every medium of communication.

The American military is the sole owner and operator of the third largest radio and TV network in the world, with 188 television stations and 27 radio stations—the majority abroad. Broadcast information specialists man these stations, and the way to become one is to ask for it. If you qualify, your training at Fort Slocum will include special emphasis on broadcasting.

If you can combine your military service with further experience in journalism, you will obviously offer greater value to future employers. Be sure to keep a scrapbook (or send things home to someone who will preserve them) to show what you have done. And then be sure to let potential employers know. Not every editor realizes the extent of practical experience in journalism that can be gained in the service.

### Moving and Money

Job changing is almost inevitable. Since there is little turnover on the editorial level at most papers, you have to improve yourself by moving up to large publications or into other media.

Moving geographically may be accomplished within your company, if it is a big one. News magazines, wire services, and larger newspapers may move you from one city bureau to another. Broadcasting networks move their newsmen up through affiliated stations into their half dozen or so owned and operated stations, and thence into New York or Washington.

What about overseas? A staff memo from one of the wire services will give you the picture in brief.

Those of you seeking Foreign Service should keep in mind that 90% of the few openings we have nowadays are in the underdeveloped countries with all the attendant personal living discomforts which not only affect you but your family as well. To get serious consideration you must have at least one foreign language.

Like Washington, the overseas assignment is an earned promotion. Fluency in a foreign language will help you get it, though you won't necessarily wind up where you'll use your language. (Just having it may help land you in London, for instance.)

Journalism today is a field in which many earn comfortable incomes but very few get rich. The salary scale moves upward from a low for newspaper and wire service employees to better pay for those on magazines and in public relations to the highest for syndicated columnists and for those who are seen on the air on television. The most attractive fringe benefits are found at magazines published by large corporations, where group insurance, retirement plans, profit sharing, and bonuses are well established.

A few figures will give you the general picture. Journalism school graduates now start at an average salary of $95 per week on their first jobs. A *New York Times* copy boy gets $61, then $91.55 when he is promoted to news clerk, and $111.25 after three years.

Columbia's 1961 graduates who went directly into broadcast or magazine jobs averaged $124 in starting salaries. American Newspaper Guild starting minimums for reporters and photographers, as of December 1, 1961, ranged from a low of $49.50 for the *Chicago Defender* (three Canadian papers were lower) to a high of $104.55 for the *New York Times*. (It is possible to start above the minimum.) A trainee in public relations gets just under $100 a week. At NBC and CBS newsrooms in New York, minimum pay for a reporter is about $175 a week. There is no room for beginners at such prices: From three to five years' experience at a major daily paper or affiliated station, or at a wire service, is expected.

How high can you go? Newspaper reporter and photographer top minimums under guild contracts run from $92.50 in the fourth year at the *Chicago Defender* to $168 in the seventh year at the *New York News*. Wire service top minimums are $161.50 in several key cities. The *New York Times* has more than 30 deskmen paid above scale, some up to nearly $300; more than 140 reporters above scale, up to nearly $350; and more than 80 editors, editorial writers, columnists and desk heads above scale, up to $500.

In public relations, a few years' experience brings
$10,000 to $12,000 a year, while a corporation public relations director earns anywhere from $15,000 to
$25,000 and seasoned PR executives may earn twice as
much.

Broadcasting on the air adds talent fees for sponsored
news programs to the experienced reporter's $300 to $400
per week; with luck and ability and several shows on the
air regularly, you can earn from $15,000 to $25,000
within a few years after graduating from college. But
remember that for every journalist who is broadcasting on
CBS, NBC, or ABC, or heading a desk at the *New York
Times*, hundreds are earning average wages. The national
average for reporters, revealed in a 1960 study by the
Associated Press Managing Editors Association, was
$7,079.

The principal unions in the business are the American
Newspaper Guild (of which the Wire Service Guild is a
part) and the Radio Writers Guild. None operates a closed
shop; you don't *have* to belong. But the guild's protection
is valuable. Bear in mind that it builds floors, not ceilings,
and that nothing in its provisions keeps an employee from
negotiating wages above scale.

The guild is not represented everywhere. Its contracts
cover about half the daily U. S. newspaper circulation and
most leading newspapers, 9 wire and news services, 19 news
and feature magazines, plus radio and TV stations and
miscellaneous publications. It numbers 32,000 members,
with local chapters in 100 cities in the United States and
Canada. When the *Los Angeles Mirror* died in 1961, it had

no guild contracts. The *Wall Street Journal* and the chain of Fairchild business publications have none.

## *Recruitment and Interviews*

Compared to industry's annual springtime invasion of college campuses, journalism will make very little effort to come looking for you. Only about twenty-five of the top newspapers do any recruiting on campuses. The Associated Press does no recruiting; the *New York Times* does none (of all papers, it least needs to) ; the television networks do none. The *Wall Street Journal* does recruit on the campus; it encourages young people who have no experience and pays them well to start. You will do well to contact nearby publications early in your senior year in college. Check back from time to time to bring your application up to date.

If you earn advancement on a college paper, or a Phi Beta Kappa key, or if you do an exceptional story that adds impressively to your scrapbook, let the man who interviewed you earlier know about it. And remember that editors lead hectic lives and have off days—so more than one appearance in an editor's office may help your cause.

The man to see is the managing editor at a paper, the news director at a station, the bureau chief at a wire service bureau—or their assistants, if the operation is large, or the personnel office if it is even larger. Your college placement office should be able to steer you toward interviews and possible openings. The classified ad columns of *Editor & Publisher*, the weekly magazine of the business, list "help wanted" all over the country.

News is gathered by asking questions, so let the man who's interviewing you know that you can express yourself. Be able to touch-type and spell. Keep a scrapbook of your best work from the student publication or from your work as a part-time stringer, and show it when you're interviewed. Show that you can work amid noise and confusion.

Newspapers need 3,500 new people a year. That's about 1,000 more than graduate from journalism school yearly, and of those an ever-smaller number go into newspaper work. One study shows that two thirds of the dailies in the United States consider the personnel shortage in their news departments as a leading problem. The problem may be their own fault, for the mass media have done a poor job of selling their career opportunities to young people. Some are beginning to wake up to this responsibility. But don't wait, if they are not stirring. Go wake them.

## TEN

## *The Future in Journalism*

EVEN THE UNITED STATES CENSUS
BUREAU has expressed surprise at the way our population
is growing. At the present rate, we will number nearly 215
million people by 1970. By the time you reach the peak of
your career in journalism in the year 2000, there may be
353 million of us. Already our biggest city is not really
New York or Los Angeles but the 500-mile megalopolis
extending from Boston to Washington that includes 38
million people.

Population growth guarantees the growth of many
businesses, including all the media of journalism, and inevitably, growth means change. Statisticians can predict
the growth; almost no one can predict all the change.
Nonetheless, based on today's evidence, let's try to look
into the future.

### The Future of the Media

Let's begin with newspapers.

"They are dying," says someone.

Some are dying. Some are consolidating. The giants in

the big cities no longer perform many of the functions they performed more than thirty years ago. Individual papers are not the political organs they once were. Where two papers are alike in content and makeup, running wire service reports that are almost identical, who needs both? Where ponderous mechanical methods date back almost to Benjamin Franklin, production and labor costs are high. And where changes in the content and makeup of the population have not been reflected in the content and makeup of the paper, it does not grow beyond the city limits with its audience. So it is true—some big city newspapers are dying.

But growth *is* occurring today—in the suburbs. While Los Angeles lost two big dailies in 1961, twenty-four other daily newspapers are prospering in Los Angeles County. They will prosper while the giant *New York Times* plunks down in their midst—for it is edited in New York for those in Los Angeles who want *Times* coverage of world and national news. The *Times* leaves it to the local papers to tell the local news; gradually, this may well be the story of major newspapers in Philadelphia, Chicago, St. Louis, and other ever-expanding cities, too. For by 1970, more than 60 per cent of the American population will be classified as suburban. Major papers that recognize the changing patterns of living, and that realize they cannot adequately cover all the local news in each suburb, will concentrate on covering the world and the nation and on providing interpretation and background in depth. Their neighbors in the suburbs will concentrate on covering the ever-increasing amount of local politics, accidents, fires, public events, social news. They will have plenty to cover—for wherever there are plenty of people, there is plenty of news.

Where the population is growing like wildfire, you find more dramatic developments. In Phoenix, 1962 saw the debut of a brand new daily newspaper, the *Arizona Journal*. With 50,000 initial circulation and a plant built to handle 250,000, it hit the streets as a full-blown metropolitan paper. Printed by photo-offset, a process in which the printing plate is made from a photograph of the complete page, its production costs run about half those of a conventional letterpress newspaper. With its banks of phototypesetter machines, which produce copy on film ready to be mounted in page form, and with computers which punch a tape to set classified ads in order, the *Journal* is the last word in modernity. But it is not alone in investing for the future. In 1961, some 832 newspapers spent $100 million on plant expansion.

Plants and machines of the future will speed the processing of news and reduce the cost of moving it from the editor's desk to the reader. Already the *New York Times* sends its copy from New York to Los Angeles at 1,000 words a minute, or 120 columns of type in an hour and a half, in the form of impulses that punch tapes for Teletypesetters. The *Times* has transmitted news at the same rate to its Paris edition, experimentally, by way of the communications satellite Telstar. Already independent weekly papers are mutually financing central publishing plants and in many of them photo-offset is saying that Linotype has seen better days.

Many journalists believe that Sunday newspapers will become more like magazines. Slimmer in size, better focused in editorial content, Sunday papers may follow the lead of the *St. Louis Globe Democrat*, which now delivers the Sunday paper as a weekend edition on Saturday morning.

Magazines, which are now not far from being able to publish on newspaper schedules, may be expected to compete with newspapers more strongly. Today, thanks to facsimile, the Chicago printer of a national magazine has his proofs corrected in New York within a few hours. Soon a magazine will be able to send complete, corrected pages electronically to printers in several different parts of the country for identical reproduction.

By 1970 the number of households buying magazines is expected to have increased by 60 per cent from 1950, while total magazine circulation will have doubled. *McCall's* expects to sell 11 million copies monthly in its regular editions by 1965. The number of business publications is expected to go from 2,275 in 1960 to 3,000 in 1970, with a distribution of 75 million copies monthly.

Television and newspapers will always be complementary to each other. No other medium can match TV for immediacy—but after the event has occurred in the living room there is a continuing urge to read more about it. When the time comes that all TV sets can tune in 83 channels (70 ultra high frequency besides today's 13 very high frequency), you may expect considerable growth in the amount of informational and documentary programing that is on the air.

Coming out of its quandary about what to do about TV, radio has caught onto the strength of local service and audiences with special fields of interest. FM's growth promises not only good music but informational and discussion programs galore. Current studies indicate that listeners switch the dial less than in the past; as radio news and information programs match those audiences, they will grow with them.

The two American wire services are now almost uniform in style, and offer parallel services. Some think they will eventually become one. But growth of wire service operations is practically guaranteed by world events and our interest and involvement in them. In 1960 over 150 newspapers were added to the list receiving AP world service. From only one bureau in all of Africa, AP on that continent has grown to six. New bureaus continue to open in Latin America.

## The Future of News

What about the future of news—and of what news is?

The world is information-hungry. The trend away from fiction in our magazines is well established, and it is now seen in television. The increase in the public taste for information is shown by the rise in magazine circulation between 1940 and 1960, when tremendous growth occurred in our population: Detective magazines went up 1.8 per cent, but news magazines grew by 257 per cent.

The growth of "think piece" magazines indicates not only that sensationalism is not necessarily the road to circulation today but that the public is eager for interpre-

tive writing. With the general level of education growing
constantly higher, there are more people who want to
know not only the fact but the truth behind the fact, who
want information more than entertainment.

One interesting indication of the future of news is a
1962 survey which showed that the believability of television news had increased by 10 per cent in two years while
the believability of newspapers had declined by 8 per cent.
Apparently people believe what they see and hear more
than what they read. News handling that is unexaggerated
and nonpartisan, and that sees events in values other than
black and white, will help the printed media regain
believability.

While science news generally is already a page-one item,
one of its branches—medicine—is coming up fast as a
subject for specialization by journalists. The American
public now spends close to $20 billion a year for medical
care; operation of hospitals is our third largest industry.
Yet a reporter with a medical education is a rarity. Already, space-age reporting is so thorough that, although
he has never been near one, the youth of today knows the
inside of an astronaut's space capsule the way his father
in the 1920's and thirties knew the inside of a Model T
Ford engine. Science is not the only area in which the
knowledge explosion will continue to be felt; housing,
education, cultural subjects are just a few of many others.

The importance of a broad general education *and* of
specialization cannot be overstressed. The need for more
interpretation calls for better writing, especially before
the microphone, where the news is not always well articu-

lated. To combine pictures and words into a context that tells a finished story will require key positions for photojournalists. The broadcasting networks now report the news faster than any other medium; for them also to gather it faster and more completely than anybody else, as they hope to do, will require larger staffs of experienced journalists in reporting, writing, and editing as well as production capacities. One indication of what's in store: CBS has named Theodore H. White, Pulitzer-Prize-winning author of *The Making of The President 1960,* as consultant on creative planning at CBS News.

Future graduates of journalism's own training programs, and of journalism schools, are sure to have a greater impact on all the media than they have had in the past. The *St. Petersburg Times* expects that most of its top executives and specialists twenty years from now will have come from its own training program. As journalism schools develop and refine research standards (and scientific research methods *can* be applied to many areas of journalism), they will learn to match the standards of the behavioral sciences and other disciplines. Attracting greater numbers of the best brains on the campus, they will have to develop more organic programs of instruction and raise not only program standards but the performance of faculty members. At the best schools, such standards and developments are already established; when others come up to them, you will find more than today's fifty or so accredited by the American Council on Education for Journalism.

## The Future Challenges

Perhaps the first challenge to journalists of the future is that of self-criticism. The press has seldom admitted that it needs criticism or reform, yet, from the establishment of standards by the best journalism schools and the leading newspapers, some form of self-criticism will inevitably arise. A national board of critics to examine the press, report on it, and recommend standards and improvements has been suggested.

Another challenge is to research the long-term needs of the press—the balance of newspaper versus broadcast news, for instance, and suburban versus big papers—and the needs of the public. This means insisting that the public get not just what it wants, in any news medium, but what it needs.

Of the challenge to dig deeper, to do more interpretive reporting and more explaining, James Reston has said, "We are making progress, but the basic problem of this country is that we are in a kind of race with our own history, and its pace is so swift that we should be going faster, we should be quicker, we should be achieving more things than we are achieving." (James Reston, "Washington and the Press," *The Press and the People*, The Fund for the Republic.)

When world news is local news, when government by press release is combined with security clamps, when journalists are not permitted access to the news of what 669 million people in China are doing, the challenge to achieve more things than we are achieving is a big one.

Yet a greater challenge lies within the challenge to help people understand history as it happens: the challenge to help them understand with feeling. Conditioned by headlines which scream, whether or not they have anything to scream about, and by bulletins every hour on the hour, we are already callous; we accept the sensational, whether it be a slaying or nuclear bomb tests in the Pacific, as the ordinary state of affairs, and we even yawn a little. More serious is the way a massive reporting of facts has become a substitute for real understanding. Artists who can marry factual knowledge to a human understanding of things are challenged to appear in journalism. As the chief communicators in our desensitized world, journalists of the future must see that the human race does not become the unfeeling race.

History is like a great circle of ripples always moving outward, increasing in circumference. Journalism is the moving radius of that circle: It must constantly extend to sweep over a larger area of human experience and knowledge. At it grows, it changes to meet the world's changes in ideas and techniques. If you are the kind who is burning to master the techniques and to understand and express the ideas, journalism's growth must be your growth.

# APPENDICES

# APPENDIX A

# Schools of Journalism
## in the United States

THE FOLLOWING is a listing of colleges
and universities in the United States accredited by The
American Council on Education for Journalism, with the
most recent date of accreditation.

ALABAMA
  Department of Journalism
  University of Alabama
  University, Ala.
    (*News-Editorial—1957*)

CALIFORNIA
  Department of Journalism
  Fresno State College
  Fresno, Calif.
    (*News-Editorial—1959*)

  Department of Journalism and Advertising
  San Jose State College
  San Jose, Calif.
    (*Advertising, News-Editorial—1959*)

Department of Communication and Journalism
Stanford University
Palo Alto, Calif.
   (*News-Editorial—1957*)

COLORADO
   College of Journalism
   University of Colorado
   Boulder, Colo.
      (*Advertising, News-Editorial—1960*)

FLORIDA
   School of Journalism and Communications
   University of Florida
   Gainesville, Fla.
      (*Advertising, Editorial-News, Radio-Television—1955*)

GEORGIA
   Henry W. Grady School of Journalism
   University of Georgia
   Athens, Ga.
      (*Advertising-Business-Public Relations, News-Editorial
      —1957*)

ILLINOIS
   Medill School of Journalism
   Northwestern University
   Evanston, Ill.
      (*Advertising, Magazine, News-Editorial, Radio-
      Television News—1962*)
   Department of Journalism
   Southern Illinois University
   Carbondale, Ill.
      (*Advertising, Community Journalism, News-Editorial—
      1961*)

College of Journalism and Communications
University of Illinois
Urbana, Ill.
  (*Advertising, News-Editorial, Radio-Television—1962*)

INDIANA
  Department of Journalism
  Indiana University
  Bloomington, Ind.
    (*News-Editorial—1962*)

  Department of Radio and Television
  Indiana University
  Bloomington, Ind.
    (*Radio-Television—1962*)

IOWA
  Department of Technical Journalism
  Iowa State University of Agriculture and Mechanic Arts
  Ames, Iowa
    (*Technical Journalism—1960*)

  School of Journalism
  State University of Iowa
  Iowa City, Iowa
    (*Advertising, Editorial Journalism, Magazine Journalism, Public Relations, Radio Journalism—1960*)

KANSAS
  Department of Technical Journalism
  Kansas State University of Agriculture and Applied
    Science
  Manhattan, Kan.
    (*Agricultural Journalism, Home Economics and Journalism, News-Editorial—1960*)

William Allen White School of Journalism and Public
    Information
University of Kansas
Lawrence, Kan.
    (*Advertising-Business, News-Editorial, Radio-*
    *Television—1960*)

KENTUCKY
    School of Journalism
    University of Kentucky
    Lexington, Ky.
       (*General Editorial—1961*)

LOUISIANA
    School of Journalism
    Louisiana State University and Agricultural and
        Mechanical College
    Baton Rouge, La.
       (*News-Editorial—1957*)

MARYLAND
    Department of Journalism
    University of Maryland
    College Park, Md.
       (*News-Editorial, Public Relations—1961*)

MASSACHUSETTS
    School of Public Relations and Communications
    Boston University
    Boston, Mass.
       (*Public Relations, Photo Journalism—1961*)

MICHIGAN
    School of Journalism
    Michigan State University
    East Lansing, Mich.
       (*Advertising, News-Editorial—1957*)

Department of Journalism
University of Michigan
Ann Arbor, Mich.
　(*News-Editorial—1956*)

Minnesota
School of Journalism
University of Minnesota
Minneapolis, Minn.
　(*Advertising-Management, News-Editorial—1956*)

Missouri
School of Journalism
University of Missouri
Columbia, Mo.
　(*Advertising-Production,　News-Editorial,　Magazine,
　Newspaper　Publishing,　Photo　Journalism,　Radio-
　Television—1962*)

Montana
School of Journalism
Montana State University
Missoula, Mont.
　(*Advertising, News-Editorial, Radio-Television—1962*)

Nebraska
School of Journalism
University of Nebraska
Lincoln, Neb.
　(*News-Editorial—1960*)

New Jersey
School of Journalism
Rutgers University
New Brunswick, N. J.
　(*Advertising, Editorial—1959*)

NEW YORK
  Graduate School of Journalism
  Columbia University
  New York, N. Y.
    (*News-Editorial—1961*)

  School of Journalism
  Syracuse University
  Syracuse, N. Y.
    (*Advertising, Magazine, News-Editorial—1962*)

NORTH CAROLINA
  School of Journalism
  University of North Carolina
  Chapel Hill, N. C.

OHIO
  School of Journalism
  Ohio State University
  Columbus, Ohio
    (*Advertising-Management, News Writing and Editing,
    Public Relations, Radio-Television Journalism (News)
    —1957*)

OKLAHOMA
  Department of Technical Journalism
  Oklahoma State University of Agriculture and Applied
    Science
  Stillwater, Okla.
    (*Agricultural Journalism, Community Journalism,
    Home Economics Journalism, Industrial Editing—
    1957*)

  School of Journalism
  University of Oklahoma
  Norman, Okla.
    (*Advertising-Business, General Editorial, Professional
    Writing, Public Relations—1957*)

OREGON
   School of Journalism
   University of Oregon
   Eugene, Ore.
     (*Advertising-Management, News-Editorial—1960*)

SOUTH CAROLINA
   School of Journalism
   University of South Carolina
   Columbia, S. C.
     (*News-Editorial—1961*)

SOUTH DAKOTA
   Department of Printing and Journalism
   South Dakota State College of Agriculture and Mechanic
      Arts,
   Brookings, S. D.
     (*Community Journalism—1956*)

TENNESSEE
   School of Journalism
   University of Tennessee
   Knoxville, Tenn.
     (*Advertising-Management, News-Editorial—1961*)

TEXAS
   Department of Journalism
   Texas Agricultural and Mechanical College
   College Station, Texas
     (*Agricultural Journalism, Community Journalism—
     1960*)

   Department of Journalism
   Texas Women's University
   Denton, Tex.
     (*News-Editorial—1957*)

School of Journalism
University of Texas
  (*Advertising, Magazine Writing and Editing, News-Editorial—1960*)


UTAH
  Department of Journalism
  University of Utah
  Salt Lake City, Utah
    (*News-Editorial—1957*)


WASHINGTON
  School of Communications
  University of Washington
  Seattle, Wash.
    (*Advertising and Management, News-Editorial, Radio-Television—1957*)


WEST VIRGINIA
  School of Journalism
  West Virginia University
  Morgantown, W. Va.
    (*Advertising-Management, News-Editorial—1962*)


WISCONSIN
  College of Journalism
  Marquette University
  Milwaukee, Wis.
    (*Advertising, News-Editorial—1957*)
  School of Journalism
  University of Wisconsin
  Madison, Wis.
    (*Advertising-Management, News-Editorial—1962*)

Department of Agricultural Journalism
University of Wisconsin
Madison, Wis.
  (*Agricultural Journalism, Home Economics Journalism
  —1962*)

# APPENDIX B

## Suggested Reading

NOTHING CAN GIVE YOU the "feel" of a business or field of interest, or give you a sense of participation as quickly as reading its special periodicals regularly. And nothing short of actual experience can give you as complete a background of knowledge as reading the best textbooks in the field, biographies and autobiographies of its leaders, and the typical works of its practitioners. The following list is by no means exhaustive, but it includes titles in many areas of journalism.

### BOOKS

AGEE, WARREN K., EDWIN EMERY, and PHILIP H. AULT, eds., *Introduction to Mass Communications.* A definitive textbook. New York: Dodd, Mead & Co., 1960.

ALSOP, JOSEPH and STEWART, *The Reporter's Trade.* A full description of the techniques of reporting the cold war era, from Washington and abroad, documented with columns written during twelve crucial years. New York: Reynal & Company, Inc., 1958.

ANTHONY, EDWARD, *O Rare Don Marquis.* The biography of a remarkable newspaperman who was also a serious poet and a humorous versifier, as well as author and playwright, and who created archy the cockroach and mehitabel the alley cat. New York: Doubleday & Company, Inc., 1962.

BAKER, STEPHEN, *Visual Persuasion: The Effect of Pictures on the Subconscious.* Tells how the experts "read" pictures; a study of the effect of pictures in the advertising field, but valuable to the press photographer, editor, or others handling photos for publication. It contains over a thousand illustrations. New York: McGraw-Hill Book Co., 1961.

BAUS, HERBERT M., *Publicity in Action.* A thorough guide to the principles and techniques of publicity. New York: Harper & Brothers, 1954.

BELL, EARL, and KENNETH CRABBE, *The Augusta Chronicle.* A bright, vivid history of a 175-year-old southern paper that gives a lively and authentic picture of newspapering. Athens, Ga.: University of Georgia Press, 1960.

BERGER, MEYER, *The Story of the New York Times.* The history of the first 100 years of the *Times,* told in great detail by a *Times* reporter and Pulitzer Prize winner who was known as "a newspaperman's newspaperman." New York: Simon and Schuster, Inc., 1951.

BERNAYS, EDWARD L., *Crystallizing Public Opinion* (reissue). First published in 1923, this book became a landmark in the evolution of public relations practice. The new edition contains an up-to-date 56-page preface. New York: Liveright Publishing Corp., 1961.

BERNSTEIN, THEODORE M., *Watch Your Language.* An excellent handbook for the writer, whether journalist or other. Used as reference or text, it provides a guide to economical, accurate, vivid writing. By the assistant managing editor of the *New York Times.* Great Neck, N. Y.: Channel Press, Inc., 1958.

BROWN, DONALD E., and JONES, JOHN PAUL, *Radio and Television News*. A definitive text in the area of broadcast news. New York: Rinehart & Company, Inc., 1957.

CANHAM, ERWIN D., *Commitment to Freedom*. The story of the *Christian Science Monitor*'s first 50 years, by one who has been a staff member and editor for two thirds of its life. Boston: Houghton Mifflin Co., 1958.

CARROLL, GORDON, ed., *History in the Writing*. A compilation of war stories by the foreign correspondents of *Time*, *Life*, and *Fortune*, as they appeared in the Luce publications. New York: Duell, Sloan & Pearce, Inc., 1945.

CATER, DOUGLAS, *The Fourth Branch of Government*. This book explores the interaction of government and the press and gives close scrutiny to the role of news in the development of government policy. Boston: Houghton Mifflin Co., 1959.

CBS NEWS, *Television News Reporting*. A practical manual describing how television news gets on the air. New York: McGraw-Hill Book Co., 1958.

CHAPELLE, DICKIE, *What's a Woman Doing Here?* The adventures of a woman combat reporter and photographer in World War II, Algeria, Hungary, Cuba, Vietnam. New York: William Morrow & Co., Inc., 1962.

CHILDS, MARQUIS, and JAMES RESTON, eds., *Walter Lippmann and His Times*. Twelve distinguished contemporaries provide evaluations of the influence of Lippmann's life and thought. New York: Harcourt, Brace & Co., 1959.

CHURCHILL, ALLEN, *Park Row*. The story of the heyday of New York newspapering and its great personalities: Joseph Pulitzer, William Randolph Hearst, James Gordon Bennett, Jr., and Charles Chapin. New York: Rinehart & Company, Inc., 1958.

*The Complete Book of Press Photography*. A comprehensive reference book on all phases of photojournalism, often used as a standard textbook. Compiled and published by the National Press Photographers Association, Inc., 235 East 45th Street, New York 17, N. Y.

Cooper, Kent, *Barriers Down.* The biography of the Associated Press by a former executive director of the AP. New York: Farrar & Rinehart, Inc., 1942.

———, *The Right to Know.* Subtitled "An Exposition of the Evils of News Suppression and Propaganda," this book is on news dissemination by governments. New York: Farrar, Straus & Cudahy, 1956.

East, P. D., *The Magnolia Jungle.* The "life, times, and education of a southern editor" who owns and edits the *Petal Paper*, Hattiesburg, Mississippi. New York: Simon and Schuster, Inc., 1960.

*Editor & Publisher Yearbook.* Published annually as "the encyclopedia of the newspaper industry," it lists every daily newspaper in the world, including names of editors and executives, circulation figures, etc. Also such relevant items as lists of books and organizations, press services, mechanical equipment.

Emery, Edwin, *The Press and America: An Interpretive History of Journalism,* 2nd ed. The relationship between the press and its environment, covering social, cultural, political, and economic aspects. New edition of an excellent text and reference book. Englewood Cliffs, N. J.: Prentice-Hall, Inc.

Emery, Edwin, and Henry Ladd Smith. *The Press and America.* A valuable one-volume reference on American newspapering, packed with information and excellent bibliographies. New York: Prentice-Hall, Inc., 1954.

Fox, Rodney, and Robert Kerns, *Creative News Photography.* This book contains the best thinking and techniques in photojournalism today, although confined to newspapering. It is well illustrated. Ames, Iowa: Iowa State University Press, 1961.

GARST, ROBERT E., and THEODORE M. BERNSTEIN, *Headlines and Deadlines*. The third edition of a valuable manual for copy editors, explaining the techniques of copy editing for beginners as well as experienced practitioners. New York: Columbia University Press, 1961.

GOLDEN, HAL, and KITTY HANSON, *Working with the Working Press*. Detailed guidance for press agents and those in public relations who work with newspapers. Dobbs Ferry, N. Y.: Oceana Publications, Inc., 1962.

HERZBERG, JOSEPH G., ed., *Late City Edition*. A better description of the techniques that produce the daily newspaper has not yet been written. Excellent as a textbook, but of broad interest to the general reader. New York: Henry Holt & Co., Inc., 1947.

HOHENBERG, JOHN, *The Professional Journalist*. Probably the best and most thorough textbook available for the beginning journalist in the newspaper field. New York: Henry Holt & Co., Inc., 1960.

LACY, DAN, *Freedom and Communications*. A lecture series surveying the challenges that face the mass media in a free society. Urbana, Ill.: The University of Illinois Press, 1961.

LIEBLING, A. J., *The Press*. A witty and accomplished critic of the press (author of "The Wayward Press" series in the *New Yorker*) surveys the "omissions, distortions, and downright fiction" in our newspapers. New York: Ballantine Books, Inc., 1961.

LINDSTROM, CARL E., *The Fading American Newspaper*. A definitive study of the decline of the big city daily, by one of America's foremost editors. New York: Doubleday & Company, Inc., 1960.

McCALL, FLOYD H., *Press Photography*. A basic survey of the field, designed for students and newcomers to a photo staff. New York: The Macmillan Co., 1961.

MOLLENHOFF, CLARK R., *Washington Cover-Up*. An experienced Washington correspondent attacks the issue of Executive secrecy from the viewpoint of the newspaper and the public. New York: Doubleday & Company, Inc., 1962.

MORRIS, JOE ALEX, *Deadline Every Minute*. A survey of fifty years of the United Press, including most of the major news events since 1907. New York: Doubleday & Company, Inc., 1957.

MOTT, FRANK LUTHER, *American Journalism: A History 1690–1960*, 3rd ed. A new edition of an authoritative history of the newspaper and magazine press, by the dean of journalism deans and teachers. New York: The Macmillan Co., 1962.

O'CONNOR, RICHARD, *The Scandalous Mr. Bennett*. A biography of James Gordon Bennett, Jr., with emphasis on his escapades and "subsidiary careers." New York: Doubleday & Company, Inc., 1962.

O'HARA, ROBERT C., *Media for the Millions*. This book deals with the process of mass communications, describing how news is selected, processed, and manufactured. New York: Random House, 1961.

PRESTON, CHARLES, ed., *The World of the Wall Street Journal*. A selection of 180 *Journal* stories that are models of excellent business and financial writing. New York: Simon and Schuster, Inc., 1959.

*Prose by Professionals*. Compiled and published by the Society of Magazine Writers from a two-year lecture series on free-lance nonfiction writing at New York University. New York: Doubleday & Company, Inc.

SCHRAMM, WILBUR, ed., *One Day in the World's Press*. Fourteen newspapers from fourteen countries, all published on the same day of world crisis: when the Suez was attacked, and Soviet tanks entered Budapest to put down the Hungarian revolution. All fourteen editions are published, nearly complete, in English translation. Palo Alto, Calif.: Stanford University Press, 1959.

SMITH, H. ALLEN, *To Hell in a Handbasket*. The autobiography of the well-known humorist, who worked his way up from cub to columnist; it gives lighthearted but revealing insight into the field. New York: Doubleday & Company, Inc., 1962.

SNYDER, LOUIS L., and RICHARD B. MORRIS, *A Treasury of Great Reporting*. A giant anthology of "literature under pressure" from the sixteenth century to our own time. New York: Simon and Schuster, Inc., 1949.

SWANBERG, W. A., *Citizen Hearst*. A best-selling autobiography of William Randolph Hearst. It achieved added distinction when it was recommended for a Pulitzer Prize in 1962 and turned down by the Columbia Board of Trustees. New York: Charles Scribner's Sons, 1961.

WECHSLER, JAMES A., *The Age of Suspicion*. The autobiography of the fighting editor and columnist of the *New York Post*. New York: Random House, 1953.

——, *Reflections of an Angry Middle-Aged Editor*. The editor of the *New York Post* describes the political and social scene, with special emphasis on the role of the press. New York: Random House, 1960.

WEINBERG, ARTHUR and LILA, eds., *The Muckrakers*. A splendid collection of the reform pieces that appeared in *McClure's, Collier's, Everybody's, American, Hampton's, Appeal to Reason*, the *Independent*, and *Cosmopolitan*, between 1902 and 1912. New York: Simon and Schuster, Inc., 1961.

WHEELER, JOHN N., *I've Got News for You.* The memoirs of a journalist who spent fifty years heading news syndicates and dealing with the leading figures of sports, literature, politics, finance, and the theater. Contains more "name dropping" per page than almost any other book in the field. New York: E. P. Dutton & Co., Inc., 1961.

WHITE, PAUL W., *News on the Air.* Although it predates television, this book was still voted the leading favorite of radio-TV teachers in a 1961 survey. New York: Harcourt, Brace & Co., 1947.

WHITE, THEODORE H. *The Making of the President 1960.* Deservedly a best-seller and Pulitzer Prize winner. Reporting how American politics works, it also gives deep insight into political reporting. New York: Atheneum Publishers, 1961.

## MAGAZINES, PERIODICALS, AND PAMPHLETS

*Columbia Journalism Review.* A quarterly "to assess the performance of journalism in all its forms, to call attention to its shortcomings and its strengths, and to help define—or redefine—standards of honest, responsible service." Published by the Graduate School of Journalism, Columbia University, New York, N. Y.

*Editor & Publisher.* The weekly magazine of the newspaper business. Address: 850 Third Avenue, New York 22, N. Y.

*Journalism Quarterly: Devoted to Research in Journalism and Mass Communication.* As its subtitle indicates, this quarterly is research-oriented and academic in point of view. More for the serious student of journalism and the theoretical minded than for the working newsman. Published by the Association for Education in Journalism with the cooperation of the American Association of Schools and Departments of Journalism and the Kappa

Tau Alpha Society. School of Journalism, University of Minnesota, Minneapolis, 14, Minn.

*National Press Photographer.* Published monthly by the National Press Photographers Association, Inc., 235 East 45th St., New York 17, N. Y.

*Nieman Reports.* Reprints, speeches, and analytical articles on journalism by practicing newsmen, from nationwide sources, as well as much critical material not previously published. Quarterly publication of the Nieman Alumni Council, 44 Holyoke House, Cambridge 38, Mass.

*Public Relations Journal.* Monthly publication of the Public Relations Society of America, 375 Park Ave., New York, N. Y.

*The Big Story,* by Balk and Whiting. This is a journalism career pamphlet produced by the Career Committee of the Chicago Headline Club of Sigma Delta Chi. It is available by writing to Fred Whiting, Medill School of Journalism, Northwestern University, Evanston, Ill.

*The Quill.* A monthly magazine devoted to journalism, published by Sigma Delta Chi, 35 East Wacker Drive, Chicago 1, Ill.

# INDEX